MINNEAPOLIS-MOLINE
FARM TRACTORS

CHESTER PETERSON JR.
AND ROD BEEMER

MBI Publishing Company

DEDICATION

To all old iron collectors, regardless of which paint they fancy.

First published in 2000 by MBI Publishing Company, 729 Prospect Avenue, PO Box 1, Osceola, WI 54020-0001 USA

MBI Publishing Company books are also available at discounts in bulk quantity for industrial or sales-promotional use. For details write to Special Sales Manager at Motorbooks International Wholesalers & Distributors, 729 Prospect Avenue, PO Box 1, Osceola, WI 54020-0001 USA.

Library of Congress Cataloging-in-Publication Data

Peterson, Chester Jr.
    Minneapolis-Moline farm tractors / Chester Peterson, Jr. and Rod Beemer.
        p. cm.
    Includes index.
    ISBN 0-7603-0625-7 (hb : alk. paper)
    1. Minneapolis-Moline tractors—History. 2. Farm tractors—United States—History. I. Beemer, Rod, II. Title.
    TL233.6.M6 P48 2000
    631.3'72'0973--dc21

On the front cover: The ultimate tractor for any Minneapolis-Moline collector, or *any* tractor collector, for that matter, is the legendary Model UDLX Comfortractor. Designed to be a car as well as a tractor, the UDLX Comfortractor was the first assembly-line cab tractor ever built. It can pull a three-bottom plow all day long, and then take the farmer's wife to town at road speeds up to 40 mph. Its comforts include a radio, hot water heater, cigarette lighter, ashtray, and mirror with a clock. This particular 1938 UDLX is one of 150 ever built.

On the frontispiece: Over the years, a wide array of signs have adorned Minneapolis-Moline dealerships. For today's collector, a neon MM sign like this one is a prime jewel for announcing "Prairie Gold" is his or her color of choice.

On the title page: During the end of the Minneapolis-Moline days, Prairie Gold yielded to the red and white of the parent organization, White Motor Corporation. These two tractors, one bearing the MM badge *and* White logo, and the other with the White name, were produced in 1969. On the left is the Minneapolis-Moline White G950 with 86 drawbar and 97 PTO horsepower, while on the right is the White A4T-1600 Plainsman with 129 drawbar and 143 PTO horsepower.

On the contents page: On this restorer's farm, patriotism is a combination of loyalty to one's country as well as one's tractor!

On the back cover: There's no doubt that on the farm pictured here, there is a farmer who appreciates Minneapolis-Moline quality and innovation! Proudly displayed between the American farmhouse and the street sign denoting MM brand loyalty is a lovingly restored 1958 445 Industrial Utility diesel model.

Edited by Lee Klancher
Designed by Bruce Leckie

Printed in Hong Kong

CONTENTS

ACKNOWLEDGMENTS

A special thanks to Roger and Marie Mohr, sons Eugene, Martin, and Gaylen, and their MM museum. They shared their time, tractors, and knowledge without hesitation or reservation.

Also a special thanks to Dennis and Joan Parker, who contributed more than they will ever know. Without their help this book would have been woefully incomplete.

Others who have shared their time and knowledge are MM collectors Donald Oliver, Stan Stamm, Ron Becker, Clinton Base, Joe Harper, Curtis Rink, and Jim Terril; Avery collectors Gregg Phillips, Russel Miner, and Jim and Betty Parker; Minneapolis collector Bill Jansen; Calvin Overlee, retired manager of tech publications at MM; Jim Janssen, retired sales division manager for MM; Lori Williamson and staff, Minnesota Historical Society Library and Archives; Mary Ann Townsend, Floyd County Historical Society; and Brent T. Sampson, test engineer, Nebraska Tractor Test Laboratory.

To those whom we may have unintentionally omitted, please accept our thanks and our apologies.

INTRODUCTION

The Minneapolis-Moline Power Equipment Company (MM) was formed in 1929 by the merger of three agricultural implement companies. All of them were maneuvering to strengthen their position in a desperate industry that had just weathered some of its most trying years. Forming the new company were Moline Implement Company (MIC), Minneapolis Steel and Machinery Company (MS&M), and Minneapolis Threshing Machine Company (MTM). In March of 1951, MM merged with the B. F. Avery and Sons Company, whose lineage dated back to 1825. This merger tied MM's roots to one of the nation's oldest firms in the agricultural equipment manufacturing business.

Unfortunately, the rich history of the Minneapolis-Moline Power Equipment Company hasn't been well documented or preserved. Many of the various companies' records were lost or destroyed during sales and mergers. This is especially true of the White Motor Corporation's purchase of MM.

Fortunately, employees with a sense of loyalty and history rescued many archival documents and images that otherwise would have disappeared.

The Minnesota Historical Society in St. Paul, Minnesota, and the Floyd County Historical Society in Charles City, Iowa, have obtained and preserved a number of company documents and images, which they make available to researchers, collectors, and other interested parties.

We have gleaned information from all of these sources. Our objective has been to give a brief historical background of the companies that formed MM and to identify all the tractors manufactured by all the companies that came under the MM banner. We hope this book will serve as an interesting and useful reference for collectors and others interested in the Minneapolis-Moline Power Implement Company and the tractors it produced.

This book is only a starting point, for there is much more information yet to be uncovered and compiled. We welcome any and all input that will correct or augment this work.

This Moline Plow Company Universal was manufactured in 1915 and is in its original condition. Its four-cylinder engine featured pressure-fed oil lubrication, and rather unique for its day, the tractor had a locking differential, electric starting, and an electric governor to regulate engine speed. A complete line of attachments was available for it.

MOLINE PLOW COMPANY AND MINNEAPOLIS THRESHING MACHINE COMPANY

The Moline Plow Company (MPC) began in Moline, Illinois, in 1852 when Henry W. Candee and Robert K. Swan formed a partnership to build fanning mills for cleaning grain.

By 1865 the company turned its attention to making plows. Much of the know-how for plow manufacturing came from Andrew Friberg, a former Deere & Company employee, who joined Candee and Swan as a partner.

In mid-1868 another partner, Stillman W. Wheelock, joined Candee, Swan & Company and infused $75,000 of capital to ease the company's severe financial problems. At this point the name was changed from Candee, Swan & Company to the Moline Plow Company.

The next step in expanding the company came when George W. Stephens became a partner and infused additional working capital. He became president of the firm in 1882. George W. died in 1902 and was succeeded as president of MPC by his son, George Arthur Stephens.

The company was tremendously successful. From 1895 to 1910, the volume of business doubled every five years with gross sales for the year ending June 30, 1913, estimated at $15 million.

During these years, "power farming" was a concept that couldn't be ignored by agricultural machinery companies if they expected to maintain a viable market share. To this end, in 1915 MPC purchased the Universal Tractor Manufacturing Company of Columbus, Ohio. The business was transferred to MPC's facilities at Moline, Illinois. The tractor design of the Universal Tractor Manufacturing Company featured two large drive wheels located in front with the engine over the front axle.

The purchase proved to be a smart move, as the company experienced record sales. The November 30, 1916, issue of *Farm Implements* lauded the operation as having the "Largest Tractor Plant In The World," stating that the Moline Plow Company's new plant covers 5 1/2 acres of floor space. The first tractor was rolled out of the new plant on July 1, 1916.

In September of 1918 the Willys-Overland Company obtained 51 percent of the stock of MPC. Frank G. Allen of Willys-Overland replaced George Stephens as president and general manager of the firm. At this time the company name was changed to the New Moline Plow Company (NMPC).

By 1921, Willys-Overland ownership had risen to 82 percent of the NMPC and a creditor's committee overtook the financial affairs of the company. New financing plans were worked out and George N. Peek assumed the presidency of the refinanced and renamed enterprise.

In 1922, the company was restructured and became the Moline Plow Company Incorporated. Between 1922 and 1923, the company again reorganized as the Moline Implement Company (MIC).

Still able to do its job of light pulling, this Universal D model could still easily draw a mower and rake for a South Dakota farmer in 1966, a half-century after it was built. *Minnesota Historical Society*

In 1923, MIC liquidated activities in the tractor, harvester, and grain drill fields. In May of 1924 the Universal tractor plant at Rock Island was put on the market with Peek resigning shortly thereafter.

These drastic measures allowed the company to survive and become a viable short-line agricultural implement manufacturer until it became part of Minneapolis-Moline.

Universal Motor Cultivator 10-12: 1914–1915

The Universal Tractor Manufacturing Company of Columbus, Ohio, was incorporated in 1914 and produced the Universal Motor Cultivator design, with the drive wheels in front and the engine over the drive wheels. The two-cylinder opposed horizontal engine was rated at 10 horsepower at the drawbar and 12 at the belt and operated at 800 to 1,200 rpm. Forward speed was 1/2 mph to 3 mph.

The Stephens Automobile

George W. Stephens became president and controlling owner of MPC in 1882. Under his leadership, the company entered the automobile business in 1915, when it began building commercial bodies to go on Ford chassis. In 1916 the Stephens Motor Works at Freeport, Illinois, began production of MPC's passenger cars.

The company's automobiles were named The Stephens Six and initially came in two models: the Model 65, which was a five- passenger touring design, and the Model 60, a roadster. In 1918 the new overhead valve six was introduced as the Salient Six and it, too, came in two styles: the three-passenger roadster, Model 70, and the Model 75, a five-passenger touring car.

The Stephens Salient Six engine had been produced by Root & Vandervoort Company (R&V) of Moline, Illinois, since its first use in 1918. MPC purchased the engine business of R&V late in 1920. At that time Moline was taking about 80 percent of this engine production for its tractors and Stephens autos.

The medium-priced Stephens automobiles had much finer body work than was ordinarily seen in the trade. Between 1918 and 1924 several additional models were introduced. Yet on July 23, 1924, the company announced that it would cease production of the Stephens automobile. Total production of the Stephens auto is placed at approximately 30,000, of which only 20 examples are known to exist.

If you visit the agricultural history displays at the Smithsonian in Washington D.C., you'll see this Moline Universal Model D. Notice that it was capable of turning soil with a two-bottom plow. *Minnesota Historical Society*

This was the predecessor to the MPC's Universal tractor. MPC had been supplying the plows that were designed for, and sold with, the Motor Cultivator.

Moline Universal: 1915–1917

MPC purchased the Universal Tractor Manufacturing Company in 1915. It is reasonable to assume that the two-cylinder model was sold from the purchase date of November 13, 1915, to July 1, 1916, when the company's new factory in Moline, Illinois, was up and running. An instruction book, dated 1918, lists a two-cylinder Model B and C.

Some sources state that the first Universal produced at the new factory used a two-cylinder engine built by Reliable Engine Company of Portsmouth, Ohio.

It's interesting to note that the colors of the Moline Universal were red and yellow—red engine and chassis and yellow implement wheels—and these same colors continued on the MM implements as long as the company made them.

Moline Universal Model D: 1917–1923

The improved four-cylinder Universal D came out in 1917 and a year later it featured, as standard equipment, an electric self-starter and an electric headlight. The engine was designed and built by Root & Vandervoort Engineering Company of Moline, Illinois.

MPC began building its own engines in early 1917, and in 1918 the engine design was a four-cylinder model featuring overhead

valves and 192 cubic inches (ci) with a 3 1/2x5-inch bore and stroke. The top governed speed was 1,800 rpm, which produced 9 drawbar and 18 belt horsepower. The Model D was rated as a two-plow unit in most soils with three-plow ability in light soil. It's possible that this was the first farm tractor with a variable speed governor.

The Universal had its own line of implements designed especially for use with the tractor. These implements included a rear carrying truck, disc harrow, grain drill, planter, lister, cultivator, mower, grain binder, corn binder, and manure spreader.

Moline Orchard Tractor

We don't know when the Orchard Model was introduced but it carried the same engine as the Model D. The main differences

Called the Minneapolis Universal Farm Motor, this tractor was built by the Universal Tractor Company of Stillwater, Minnesota, for the Minneapolis Threshing Machine Company. It was in the Minneapolis line from 1911 to 1914. Advertised horsepower was 20 at the drawbar and 40 on the belt. *Minnesota Historical Society*

were the height of the tractor, wheel size, and crop clearance. On the Orchard version the top of the radiator was 55 1/2 inches high, which was 18 inches lower than the Model D. Wheels for the Orchard Model were 44 inches compared to 52 inches, and crop clearance was 18 inches on the Orchard tractor versus 29 1/2 inches for the Model D. Part of the package included a tool roll with a complete set of tools and an oil can.

Moline Road Tractor

Again we don't know the date the Road Tractor was introduced but it also featured the same engine as the Model D. Advertisements state it could be fitted with grader and one-yard scraper units that were capable of handling all road-building projects.

The Road Tractor could also be fitted with a heavy scarifier.

Heavy cast-iron road wheels were standard, taking the tractor to advertised speeds up to 3 miles per hour.

A product that MPC introduced at a very bad time was a 1 1/2-ton truck. According to the January 1921 issue of the *Automobile Trade Journal*, production of the truck at the Moline, Illinois, plant had just begun so it's likely that the trucks were first produced in late 1920.

The trucks were marketed through the existing MPC tractor and implement dealerships. One of the features touted was that the truck engine was the same as the tractor engines and all parts were interchangeable. This meant that repair parts for the truck were readily available at MPC's dealerships.

The *Automobile Trade Journal* article lists the following features as standard equipment: truck cord pneumatic tires, chrome vanadium springs, nickel steel gears, demountable radiator core, self-aligning dry plate clutch, rubber bumpers, strong pressed steel fenders, automatic mechanical-type governor, durable three-piece pressed steel hood, high-tension magneto with automatic impulse starter, tool kit, spare tire carrier, and odometer. Extras included electric lights, generator and starter, and a PTO assembly with 12-inch pulley.

Another product, which fared better, was the Moline Two Row Tractor Cultivator Adapter Kit for the Fordson tractor. How many were actually sold isn't recorded and it is unclear just when it was introduced, but the company's *Flying Dutchman Yearbook* of

12

It may not have been sleek and, like many tractors of its day, the radiator was positioned parallel with the frame, but the Minneapolis new 40 was so named because it produced 40 drawbar and 80 belt horsepower from its four-cylinder horizontal engine with 7 1/4x9-inch bore and stroke. *Minnesota Historical Society*

1929 lists, with details, the specifics about the kit. The *Yearbook* explains that it included rear axle extensions, fenders, and hardware to mount a single front wheel to the tractor, making it a row-crop unit for cultivation. If the artist's rendering of the product was accurate, all the parts in the kit were painted bright red.

The relentless demand for Universal tractors disappeared during the postwar recession and financial woes undermined the company until 1922. At that time, in an effort to weather the storm, it was restructured and incorporated as the Moline Plow Company, Incorporated. Between 1922 and 1923 many of the company's assets were

sold. Tractor, harvester, and drill production were liquidated in 1923, and the company again reorganized as Moline Implement Company (MIC).

In May of 1924 the Universal tractor plant at Rock Island was put on the market. Peek resigned shortly thereafter. Deere & Company seriously considered buying the MPC facility, but decided the price was too high. Instead, its archrival International Harvester Company purchased the entire plant and properties to expand its own tractor production. These drastic measures allowed the former MPC to survive and become a viable short-line agricultural implement manufacturer until it became part of MM.

Minneapolis Threshing Machine Company

The history of the Minneapolis Threshing Machine Company stretches back to the Fond du Lac Threshing Machine Company of Fond du Lac, Wisconsin. The firm began in 1874 as a manufacturer of threshers for the local farm trade. The new company failed in 1876 and John S. McDonald, one of the original investors in the venture, reorganized the company in 1877 as the McDonald Manufacturing Company.

McDonald was soon successful enough to gain the attention of investors from the Minneapolis–St. Paul area who, in April of 1877, founded a new corporation called the

There's Horsepower, and Then There's Horsepower

How many "horses" does your tractor have? That's not an easy question to answer. It depends on tests and terminology such as drawbar horsepower, belt horsepower, PTO horsepower, observed horsepower, brake horsepower, and engine horsepower, not to mention gross engine horsepower, net engine horsepower, adjusted horsepower, and SAE horsepower.

First, horsepower is a foot-pound-per-second unit of power. It's the power required to raise 550 pounds one foot in one second. This unit of measurement is said to have originated with James Watt when he was looking for a way to measure the amount of power available from ponies that were used to raise coal from coal mines. He observed that a mine pony could do 22,000 foot-pounds of work in a minute. Perhaps accounting for a full-sized horse, he added 50 percent and came up with the figure of 33,000 foot-pounds that one horse could work in one minute. Divide this figure by 60 seconds and you have the 550 foot-pounds per second.

The horsepower produced by a tractor's engine, at the tractor's drawbar, or at the tractor's PTO, is measured and expressed in several different ways as a means for owners and buyers to judge how much work the tractor can be expected to do for them. In 1920 the Nebraska Tractor Testing Laboratory at Lincoln, Nebraska, began testing tractors according to the Agricultural Tractor Test Code approved by the American Society of Agricultural Engineers and the Society of Automotive Engineers. These tests have become the standard for horsepower testing and rating of agricultural tractors.

The following are some of the various terms used when expressing horsepower ratings:

Gross horsepower is the power available at the flywheel of an engine equipped with only the parts needed to make the engine operational.

Net brake horsepower is measured at the flywheel of a fully equipped engine, which is capable of operating by itself.

Drawbar horsepower is the power available at the drawbar for pulling implements. This will be 10–15 percent lower than gross or net engine horsepower because some engine power is used to move the tractor and operate the unit's component systems, such as hydraulics, the electrical system, and others.

Belt horsepower is taken on a belt driven from the tractor's belt pulley. The power generated from a belt is less than from the PTO shaft because 1–2 percent is lost to slippage on the pulley. Belt horsepower tests were conducted at Nebraska until 1959.

PTO horsepower is measured at the tractor's power take-off. Nebraska tests are conducted with the tractor stationary. PTO tests weren't begun at Nebraska until 1960.

SAE horsepower is the Society of Automotive Engineers formula to determine the approximate brake horsepower of an engine. The SAE rating is 75 percent of the adjusted drawbar horsepower and 85 percent of the adjusted belt/PTO horsepower. This method of horsepower rating was discontinued at Nebraska in approximately 1960.

Observed brake horsepower is the power developed by an engine under the actual air, temperature, humidity, and barometric pressure conditions during the time the test is conducted.

Corrected brake horsepower is the observed brake horsepower corrected to account for altitude, temperature, humidity, and barometric pressure. The tests are corrected to 60 degrees Fahrenheit and 30 inches of mercury.

To really know how many horses a tractor has you have to know who conducted the tests and what kind of horsepower tests were used to establish the rating. In this book we have used two types of test results: observed Nebraska tests and factory observed tests. Horsepower ratings given in this book should be considered factory observed unless stated as a Nebraska test result. The ratings are truncated, or rounded down, to the nearest whole number with no decimal points or fractions given.

Early tractors frequently, if not always, acquired their model designation by adding the drawbar and belt horsepower figures to "Model," such as Twin City Model 20-35.

The company horsepower ratings arrived at prior to Nebraska's standardized testing procedures may be suspect, as many tractors were re-rated as a result of Nebraska tests.

Today tests conducted at a company's factory generally follow the same methods as those used at the Nebraska Tractor Test Laboratory.

Minneapolis Threshing Machine Company. Part of the deal was moving the company to the Twin Cities area, with a new factory building to be constructed in Hopkins, Minnesota, and corporate offices located in neighboring Minneapolis.

The deal was struck and, according to McDonald's son's memoirs, the machinery was moved to the new location in September of 1887.

Steam traction engines sold at a brisk pace and company directors soon voted to begin manufacturing steam traction engines. The initial 1892 production scheduled called for 250 steam traction engines. Late that year, the projections for the company's product looked exceptionally strong, so the production numbers for 1893 were set at 500 steam traction engines.

The panic of 1893 brought an abrupt end to the boom years. But, by stubborn resolve, management held the company together until conditions eased in 1899. McDonald, who had foreseen the demise of the steam traction engine, was voted out of the presidency in 1897.

The company prospered during the first decade of the new century, despite the fact that the market was changing from steam to gasoline power. Prior to 1911, it appears that MTM marketed a tractor with an Espe-designed two-cylinder cross-mounted engine. This unit was manufactured by the Universal Tractor Company of Stillwater, Minnesota, and was known as the Universal 20-40.

In 1913, MTM erected its own facility to build tractors, and its own Model 25-50, Model 40-80, and Model 20-40 were soon in production. Minneapolis tractors were moderate sellers.

Minneapolis Farm Motor 25-50: 1911–1914

Walter J. McVicker and the McVicker Engineering Company designed the Model 25-50 that was manufactured by the Northwest Thresher Company of Stillwater, Minnesota. This was the first of the famous Minneapolis Farm Motors. A contract for 25 tractors was made in 1911 and 48 were ordered for 1912. These units used a cross-mount four-cylinder vertical engine with a 6x8-inch bore and stroke governed at 530 rpm. Early models used a tubular radiator

The predecessor to the gas tractor, this restored Minneapolis steam traction engine is building steam at the Penfield, Illinois, tractor show. This engine was purchased new in 1921 to power a sawmill near Lincoln, Illinois. The unit weighs 32,000 pounds and carries a 24 horsepower rating. It came from the factory capable of burning wood, coal, or straw. The firebox was designed to accommodate a rack for burning straw if that was the owner's choice of fuel.

with an induced draft from the engine exhaust system. A new radiator was adopted in 1912.

Universal 20-40:1911–1914

Universal Tractor Company of Stillwater, Minnesota, built this tractor, which was also sold by other companies under other badges and names. Two such companies were the Skibo Tractor Company and Rumely, which sold it as the "GasPull." A 1912 MTM catalog states that in 1911 over 500 units were sold and that the tractor had "been in operation for two or three years," indicating that the Model 20-40 may have been offered as early as 1909 or 1910.

Power was provided by a two-cylinder opposed design engine with a 7 1/2x8-inch bore and stroke. Since this is believed to be the same tractor as the Advance-Rumely "GasPull," there is some confusion about who designed the tractor. From Rumely's historical account it is believed that O. E. Espe was the designer. It is possible that Espe

worked for the McVicker company and designed the tractor while an employee at that firm.

Minneapolis 40-80: 1912–1920

The Model 40-80 looked like a steam traction engine's next-of-kin. The rear wheels were 85 inches tall with 30-inch faces, while the front wheels were a mere 40 inches high with 14-inch faces. The tractor had chain steering like the steamers and weighed 21,000 pounds.

Everything about this unit was big, including the engine. The four-cylinder horizontal flathead had a 1,486-ci displacement from a 7 1/4x9-inch bore and stroke running at 500 rpm. In 1919 the engine was changed to an overhead valve (OHV) design.

This huge machine had two forward and one reverse speeds with the forward range from 2 to 2 3/4 miles per hour. However, the Model 40-80, which was also designed as a road engine, often had only a single forward

Detail of a restored Minneapolis steam traction engine showing it as Engine No. 8496, which was one of 71 Minneapolis steam traction engines built by the company in 1921 when the company was making the transition to gasoline tractors. The engine's governor is visible just behind the stack.

gear. Another strange feature of the Road Tractors was that the engines were counter-rotating to the agricultural tractor engines. MTM, like other tractor builders, found a ready market for machines to help build the country's roadways.

The first Model 40-80s had an open wooden cab but almost no fenders. In 1914 full metal fenders were added to the cab.

Minneapolis 35-70: 1920–1929

Some changes occurred to the Model 40-80 in 1919. The engine was changed to an OHV design and the rpm was upped to 550. The rest of the tractor remained much the same. Then, as a result of Nebraska test number 15 in May and June of 1920, the Model 40-80 was re-rated to the Minneapolis Model 35-70. Actual results of the test were 52 drawbar and 74 belt horsepower.

These kerosene engines were started on gasoline, from a small auxiliary tank, and once the engine temperature reached sufficient levels, switched to run on kerosene. Water was added as an antiknock agent when the engine was operating under a heavy load.

Minneapolis 20-40: 1916–1919

Patterned after the Model 40-80, the Minneapolis Model 20-40 had a cross-mounted four-cylinder flathead engine of 5 3/4x7-inch bore and stroke running at 650 rpm. The cooling system was of the automotive type with a radiator fan. The two-speed transmission produced forward travel at 2 and 2 1/4 miles per hour..

Minneapolis 22-44: 1920–1927

Re-rated from the Model 20-40 in 1920, the engine design of the Model 22-44 was changed to OHV, and the bore was enlarged 1/4 inch to give the new design a 6x7-inch bore and stroke. The rpm remained at 650 until 1921, when raised to 700. Nebraska test number 14 gave the drawbar horsepower as 33 and the belt horsepower as 46.

The transmission became a 2/1 with forward speeds of 1.98 and 2.6 miles per hour and reverse at 1.98 miles per hour.

Minneapolis 15: 1915–1917

When it was first introduced in late 1915, the Model 15 was available with either one front wheel or two front wheels on a standard-type front axle. At the back, until 1917, only one of the rear wheels was a driver. On the 1917 model you could engage the other drive wheel via a hand clutch. However, there wasn't any differential so it was necessary to disengage the second driver rear wheel to corner.

In 1918 it received some engineering changes and the Model designation became the 15-30.

Minneapolis 15-30: 1918–1919

The 1918 Model 15-30 was an improved Model 15 and had two rear drivers and two front wheels.

The engine was a 445-ci four-cylinder with 4 1/2x7-inch bore and stroke which operated at 750 rpm. In 1920 the 15-30 became the Model 12-25 as a result of test number 13 conducted at Nebraska. The test showed 16 drawbar and 26 belt horsepower.

Minneapolis 12-25: 1919–1924

Some sources list this tractor as being in production through 1926, but it disappears from the MTM catalogs in 1924. Regardless of production dates, it used the same engine throughout its many changes and was tested at Nebraska in 1920, when it acquired the 12-25 rating.

Minneapolis 17-30: 1921–1926

The engine for the Model 17-30 had the crankcase and block cast as one piece, which became part of the tractor's frame. This approach was similar to the Fordson and other brands that were moving toward the "unit frame" design.

It was a four-cylinder vertical crossmount with 4 3/4x7-inch bore and stroke operating at 775 rpm. Nebraska test number 70, conducted in 1921, gave the tractor ratings of 19 drawbar and 31 belt horsepower. This model was designated the "A" when the "B" was brought on-line in 1926.

Minneapolis 17-30A: 1926–1934

The 496-ci OHV engine used on the 17-30 was also used on this tractor but the rpm was upped to 825. The Model 17-30A tractor was advertised as a three-plow machine.

Two forward and one reverse gears moved the unit at 2 to 2.7 miles per hour and 2.7 miles per hour, respectively.

Minneapolis 17-30B: 1926–1934

Advertised as a four-plow tractor, the "B" had a slightly larger bore, 4 7/8 inches instead of 4 3/4 inches, and the gearing allowed faster ground speeds of 2.3 and 3 miles per hour. Horsepower on the "B" was recorded as 23 drawbar and 34 belt when Nebraska test number 118 was conducted in 1925.

The frame for the "B" was 10 inches longer than that of the "A." Rear wheels on both models were 53 inches in diameter with 12-inch faces fitted with spade lugs, which were standard equipment. An option on both the "A" and "B" tractors was a 527-rpm PTO.

It appears that a considerable number of the Model 17-30Bs were marketed in 1925, although they didn't show up in the company's catalog until 1926.

Minneapolis 27-42: 1929

This was the same tractor as the Model 17-30B, only governed at a faster rpm. Just when the Model 27-42 was dropped from the line is uncertain. It appeared in the first MM 1929 catalog but in all probability lasted only one year.

The crossmount vertical OHV engine had 522 ci and 4 7/8 x7-inch bore and stroke turning 925 rpm. The 2/1 transmission allowed forward speeds of 2.7 and 3.4 miles per hour.

A Model 27-42 with serial number 9044 was tested at Nebraska in 1929. The results were 34 drawbar and 48 belt horsepower.

Minneapolis 39-57, 30-50: 1928–1929

A repair parts list, number R802, for the Minneapolis 39-57 states that this tractor was formerly the Model 30-50. No other information on a Model 30-50 came to light during our research.

This tractor didn't use an MTM engine, but rather a Stearns four-cylinder I-head with 5 1/2x6 1/2-inch bore and stroke giving a total displacement of 617 ci. It operated at a governed speed of 1,000 rpm.

The 2/1 transmission gave forward speeds of 3 and 3.9 miles per hour. Immediately after the merger of MTM, MIC, and MS&M in 1929, this tractor apparently became a joint effort between MTM's Hopkins plant and the Lake Street facility of MS&M because it contains many Twin City parts. An "R" prefix in the serial number is believed to indicate a rebuilt unit. MTM had a policy of taking its used tractors back to the factory and rebuilding them.

The postwar recession hurt MTM's finances, and were further imperiled by Ford's tractor price war. As the 1920s drew to a close, MTM was laboring under $2,000,000 of bank debt that refused to go away.

To make matters even worse, the plant was in need of major improvement to keep producing a high-quality tractor. It was at this critical time that the company learned of the impending merger of MS&M and MIC. Instead of viewing this union as an ominous competitive threat, the company saw it as an opportunity. MTM asked to be included in the merger. Officials at the other two companies saw advantages in MTM's proposal. The negotiations were expanded and executives and owners of all three companies reached an agreement. On April 18, 1929, MTM became part of the Minneapolis-Moline Power Implement Company.

When the Nebraska Tractor Tests in 1926 showed 12-20s like this 1925 model had more than their stated power of 12 drawbar and 20 belt horsepower, it was quickly renamed the 17-28 Y to more accurately report its greater oomph.

MINNEAPOLIS STEEL AND MACHINERY COMPANY

MS&M was organized in 1902 by three men who had been successful at other manufacturing endeavors in the Minneapolis area.

J. L. Record was retired president of Barnett & Record, a firm that had built hundreds of grain elevators along the railroads of the Dakotas and Montana. Record became president of MS&M at its inception.

O. P. Briggs and E. A. Merrill had been with the Twin City Iron Works, which manufactured Corliss engines and supplied them as power plants in new flour mills, local light plants, water works, and so on, for new towns and communities that sprang up with the westward expansion. Briggs became vice president of MS&M and Merrill became treasurer.

L. S. Gillette and his brother, R. P. Gillette, had been associated with, and retired from, the steel fabrication enterprise Gillette-Herzog Manufacturing Company. L. S. had served as president of that company. Gillette-Herzog fabricated the steel for many of the larger buildings and bridges in Minneapolis and St. Paul, and also supplied steel for municipal water towers, lamp posts for street lights, and many other items needed to build new communities. The brothers retired when the company was sold to the American Bridge Company. R. P. Gillette became secretary of MS&M.

These individuals brought a wealth of manufacturing knowledge to Minneapolis Steel and Machinery Company at the dawn of the gasoline tractor era.

Just when MS&M entered the tractor market isn't exactly clear. C. H. Wendel's *Encyclopedia of American Farm Tractors* states that "Possibly as early as 1906 Walter J. McVicker designed a gas tractor having a 9x12-inch bore and stroke and contracted with MS&M to have the tractor built."

Another source has this to say about the early McVicker tractor: "About 1908, W. J. McVicker, engineer, brought the drawings to the factory for the Joy-Wilson tractor and two of those were made. There were four-cylinder engines on these tractors with a 10x10-inch bore and stroke. Tractors were chain driven, wheels 30" face and about 9' in diameter, traveled about 2 miles per hour and pulled twelve to sixteen plows. One engineer that worked on these tractors, the late J. C. Junkin, later designed the Twin City '40' the first one of which was produced in 1910, and this Twin City '40' early made a reputation pulling a Giant plow in South Texas, breaking up mesquite roots to clear the lands that are now raising enormous cotton crops in the Corpus Christi district on such ranches as the Taft Ranch at Gregory and King Ranch at Kingsville." The quote is from a paper titled "Minneapolis-Moline History" filed in the Minnesota Historical Society archives.

Additional information on this first tractor design is found in R. B. Gray's *The Agricultural Tractor 1855-1950*. "Apparently in 1909 the McVicker Engineering Company designed a large tractor for the Joy-Wilson Sales Company of Denver, Colorado. The tractors following this design were built in

The 12-20 exhaust system has no muffler. The restorer remembers that at night the hot exhaust manifold would become cherry red. He says that, not surprisingly, it was also an extremely noisy tractor.

the shops of the Minneapolis Steel and Machinery Company of Minneapolis, Minnesota, under the name of Joy-McVicker."

MS&M was also exploring the stationary steam engine market but it soon switched its focus to gasoline-powered units. From 1906 to 1910 it sold gasoline engines to firms such as J. I. Case Threshing Machine Company of Racine, Wisconsin, and Reeves & Company of Columbus, Indiana. The latter company used

the engines in its own 40-horsepower tractor.

Encouraged by the ready market for the tractors it had built for other companies, MS&M developed its own "Twin City Forty" (40-65) and placed it on the market in 1910. Over the next decade the company put out a number of new models.

In 1913 the 25-45 tractor was introduced, which was similar in construction to the Twin City 40-65. The next year, 1914, MS&M

brought to market its Twin City 60-90, based on the 40-65. The 60-90 was outfitted with a six-cylinder engine, while the 40-65 used a four-cylinder version of the same power plant.

Further tractor developments included an all-enclosed automotive-type design designated the Twin City 16-30, introduced in 1917. This was followed in 1919 by the Twin City 12-20 (later rated 17-28), and in 1920 the Twin City 20-35 (rated 27-44 in 1926) was introduced into the line.

The MS&M annual reports show the rapid growth of the tractor program. The company's 1911 report breaks the firm's operations into two groups, the structural department and the mechanical department. The structural department covered mill buildings, office and other buildings, tanks, towers, elevators, highway bridges, railroad bridges, and miscellaneous shop work. Tractors were in the mechanical department, which also included gas engines, Corliss engines, transmission machinery, and miscellaneous shop work.

In 1911 the company charged $9,640.96 against experimental work on the Twin City "Forty" tractor. Projected production on gas traction engines for the following year was set at 200 to 250 units. The annual report also discloses a recent contract to manufacture 500 gas tractors for a "large implement house." The following year's report identifies the buyer as the J. I. Case Threshing Machine Company.

The author of the report for 1912 indicates, "In the Machinery Department we have actual sales for future delivery, aggregating $500,000 as against $97,000 a year ago; a large percentage being the uncompleted portion of the Case contract and the motors we are furnishing Reeves & Company."

Near the end of 1912, the company entered a contract with Deere & Company to handle MS&M's Twin City tractors in all foreign countries except Canada. The annual report confidently tells shareholders, "There is no doubt, at the expiration of the Case contract, the demand for our own machines will occupy our full capacity."

The 1913 annual report discloses yet another important contract, this one to make a large number of tractors for the Bull Tractor Company. The contract brought MS&M an aggregate total of $1,000,000. The units were in production at the time of the report, and were soon to be "put into actual service for a thorough test, after which, if the machine proved satisfactory, manufacture would proceed at a rapid rate."

During 1914 the company developed a Twin City Twentieth Century Tractor, "a three-wheel, three-plow, moderate priced machine." After testing and demonstrations at shows, MS&M made a five-year contract to meet the tractor requirements of the Grain Growers' Grain Company of Canada, an association of some 40,000 farmers. Orders for Bull Tractors, Twentieth Century Tractors, Twin City motors, and other goods totaled $1,800,000 at this time.

The company's 1915 report states that "its own Tractor business and the Tractor business generally is on a better basis than ever before and the Company has found, and is finding, ready market for all that it can turn out."

The outlook the following year was just as strong. The company built 2,600 Bull Tractors in 1916 and a large number of Twin City tractors. It never had enough tractors to fill orders. At the start of 1917, the company had contracts for another 2,000 Bull Tractors and more Twin City tractors and motors than in the previous year.

World War I turned much of the company's production facilities to military munitions and war materiel contracts. During this period, tractor manufacturing for other companies was abandoned and the company's own tractor program was maintained with some difficulty.

The country's railroads deteriorated during the war, and once the conflict was over the rolling stock was in need of extensive repair and overhaul. MS&M officials saw in the aging rail system a use for its own increased production capacity. The company negotiated contracts with three Twin Cities railroads in August and September 1922, and turned one-third of the MS&M plant into a locomotive repair shop. By the end of that year, the plant could accommodate 25 locomotives at a time. This work helped the company weather the recession following the war, after which the structural steel business rebounded and the tractor program gained momentum.

In 1920 the company was producing five Twin City models: the 12, 16, 25, 40, and 60.

The 12-20s were delivered with steel wheels that either had spade lugs or angle lugs like those on this unit. Its production run from 1919 to 1926 was several years before rubber tires were available on farm tractors.

But by 1929, the year of the consolidation, the market for the larger sizes had disappeared and the company was building the Model 17-28, the Model 21-32, and the Model 27-44. The old Model 12-20, introduced during the war years, had become the Twin City Model 17-28 of 1929. Throughout all the years of its production, this was one of the most popular tractors with the nation's farmers.

Joy-McVicker 50-140: 1911

There is some confusion about who ordered, and who designed, this tractor. Some sources say it was designed by the McVicker Engineering Company of Minneapolis, Minnesota, for the Joy-Wilson Sales Company of Denver, Colorado, and built by the MS&M Company. What is apparent is that they carried the Joy-McVicker badge.

Another source, *Minneapolis-Moline: A History of its Formation and Operations,* by Norman F. Thomas, gives this account of the tractor's development: "A contract was signed (author's note—probably late 1910) with Joy-Wilson Company of Minneapolis to develop the new tractor and in February that company ordered five 'gas traction engines.' The drawings were completed by McVicker Engineering Company in November and

Paint Scheme Guidelines

Moline Plow Company

The entire tractor was red, including the front wheels. The rear truck wheels and the implement wheels, however, were yellow—not too different from Prairie Gold. After the merger, MM chose to continue this paint scheme on its tillage implements until the end of MM company production.

Minneapolis Threshing Machine Company

The "Great Minneapolis" tractors had gray engines and chassis, light gray tin work, green cabs and fenders, and red wheels.

Minneapolis Steel and Machinery Company

Early, heavy Twin City tractors had green power units, silver radiators, and dark red frames and wheels. Starting with the Model 16, the color was changed to all dark gray until 1938, when the Twin City–type tractors sported red wheels.

Minneapolis-Moline Power Implement Company

Beginning with the Model Z tractors the golden yellow color known as Prairie Gold was introduced. Early original Prairie Gold tractor parts that haven't been repainted suggest that the early yellow color tended to be a much less bright orange than the later Prairie Gold color. In fact, early company advertisements didn't use the term "Prairie Gold" to describe the tractor's color scheme. The change to the bright orange now referred to as Prairie Gold didn't occur until after World War II, probably about 1948. This Prairie Gold paint color was used until the end of Model 335, Model 445, 5 Star, and Model GB production, with the exception of the late Industrial models.

The 4 Star, Model M5, and Model GVI had a new shade of darker Prairie Gold tin work and wheels with metallic bronze chassis. The first-series Jet Stars were entirely metallic bronze with Prairie Gold wheels.

The Jet Star 2, Jet Star 3, U302, M602, M604, M607, G705, and G706 models featured the lighter Energy Yellow tin work and wheels with Dyna Brown chassis and a small white band around the grilles. This color scheme also included the following models: Jet Star 3 Super, U302 Super and M670 Super through 1966, G707, G708, and the G1000. A white band encompassed the hoods of these tractors, providing a background for the company name lettering.

Beginning in 1967 models of the Jet Star 3 Super, U302 Super, M670 Super, G900, G1000 Vista, and the late-production G1000 Wheatland were entirely Energy Yellow.

The 50 Series and 55 Series were entirely Energy Yellow, except on these models the wheels were white. The white hood band was also seen on this series.

Paying homage to the company's long and celebrated history, MM and Oliver adopted an optional red, white, and blue Heritage color scheme for some 1969 and 1970 model tractors. Heritage tractors also had five blue stars on the fenders.

Heritage colors were available on the 550, 750, 850, 940, 950, 1050, 1350, and the A4T. The A4T also carried the name Plainsman when painted the Heritage colors. The 950, 1050, and 1350 models could also carry a red, white, and black paint job. These weren't considered Heritage models, and few vehicles came off the assembly line in these colors.

The A4T tractor's standard production colors were red, white, and black with the exception of the Heritage models.

---

management ordered two tractors to be finished for field tests for February 1911, and three more finished for March."

Two of these tractors were sold in South America at $2,560 each. The huge machines weighed 18,000 pounds and were powered by a four-cylinder vertical engine operating at 250 rpm.

We found no record of whether MS&M built more than the original five machines, although the company did redesign the model, which became the Twin City 40. Company records suggest nearly $10,000 was spent on this redesign work.

Twin City 40-65: 1912–1924

MS&M-built engines were used on the Twin City 40-65 mounted lengthwise on the frame. They were a vertical L-head with 7 1/4x9-inch bore and stroke, giving 1,486-ci displacement and operating at 500 rpm.

The engine wasn't the only big feature of this tractor. It weighed 23,700 pounds and the rear wheels stood 84 inches high with 24-inch faces. It could move either forward or reverse at 2 miles per hour.

During its lifetime it used two different radiator designs. Also during its evolution the bore was increased to 7 3/4 inches, the engine design was changed to OHVs, and the rpm was increased to 535. This was tagged the Type B engine and the 7 1/4-inch model became known as the Type A engine.

The Army Engineering Corps used some of the Twin City 40-65 tractors to move heavy equipment and perform other duties requiring high horsepower.

Twin City 25-45: 1913–1920

Of the same basic design as the Model 40-65, this tractor utilized three different engine designs throughout its lifetime. The Model A with serial numbers 2501-2646 was a horizontal crossmount engine with 6x8-inch bore and stroke. The Model B with serial numbers 2647-2673 was a vertical crossmount design with the same 6x8-inch bore and stroke.

Another change was made at serial numbers 2701-2797 when it became the Model C with the same vertical engine mounted lengthwise on the frame.

The Model D, serial numbers 2801-2815, apparently used the same engine as the

Contemporaries meet again. The 12-20 Twin City came off the assembly line in 1923 and the Ford Model T was made in 1925. Henry Ford became famous stressing that buyers of his Model Ts could have any color they wanted—as long as it was black. The Model T sold for $295 F.O.B. Detroit, Michigan, slightly more than half the cost of the tractor.

Model C. The change in model designation suggests there were some differences that didn't appear in our research.

The next—and last—change was the Model E with a larger, 6 1/4x8-inch bore and stroke, carrying serial numbers 2816–3126. It is believed that the engine rpm on all models was 600.

Transmission was a 1/1 geared for travel either way at 2 1/2 miles per hour.

Twin City 15-30: 1913–1917

A serial number list from the archives of the Minnesota Historical Society lists the TC 15-30 as having serial numbers 5001–5478 with TD and TF engines. Unfortunately it doesn't give production dates.

Other sources state that three different versions of the Model 15-30 were built. The earlier models used a small, horizontal crossmount engine. Later, the crossmounted engine was replaced with a vertical inline design still using the tubular-style radiator of the early model.

In 1917 the inline engine had a 4 3/4x7-inch bore and stroke governed at 650 rpm. It appears that sometime in 1917, probably late, the tubular radiator was changed to an automotive-type cellular design.

The only transmission information found was a 2/1 giving forward speeds of 1 3/4 and 2 1/2 miles per hour.

Twin City Twentieth Century: 1914–1919

Just when production of the 15 horsepower "Twentieth Century" stopped is unknown. MS&M signed a five-year contract with the Grain Growers' Company of Canada sometime in 1914. Whether or not production continued through all the following five years is questionable because Thomas's work, quoted previously, lists only four models of tractors being produced by the company in 1917.

The Twentieth Century Model, a three-wheel three-plow tractor, appeared enough like the Bull tractor—which MS&M was manufacturing—that the Bull Company asked MS&M to promise not to sell the new "Twentieth Century" model in the United States for one year.

The Bull tractor was in production during 1914, using three different engines supplied by the Bull Company. First production used engines from Ludington. When production outstripped available supply from that source, 1,000 engines were ordered from Buda, and finally Toro was asked to become an additional supplier of engines.

Since engines from the above manufacturers were in short supply, it seems likely that MS&M would have used its own power plant in the "Twentieth Century" tractors although we were unable to confirm this.

Twin City 60-110: 1913–1915

Here is another tractor that has produced a confusing pedigree. R. B. Gray in his book, *The Agricultural Tractor 1855-1950,* states that the 60-110 was re-rated as the 60-90 in 1916, no doubt pursuant to further testing. To further confuse the issue, a document in the Minnesota Historical Society archives mentions a Model 60-95 version of this tractor. It was the only place we found of reference to this third tractor. This document, however, lists the Model 60-90 and Model 60-95 as being of earlier production than the Model 60-110.

What is rather certain is that the engine was a vertical six-cylinder design with 7 1/4x9-inch bore and stroke operating at 500 rpm. The Bennett carburetor allowed operation on gasoline, kerosene, or distillates. Cooling was via the familiar Twin City tubular-style radiator. The operator had the choice of moving the giant 27,700-pound vehicle forward or backward at 2 miles per hour. The rear wheels measured 84 inches tall with 30-inch faces.

Twin City 60-90: 1916–1921

Thomas's work, previously quoted, lists the "60" as one of the four tractors in production in 1917. Yet it doesn't specify which of the 60 models it refers to. On the other hand, the February 14, 1918, issue of *Automotive Industries* states that the six-cylinder Model 60-90 with 7 1/4x9-inch bore and stroke was one of four tractor models currently in production at MS&M.

The engine, and many of the other features of the Model 60-90, have been discussed under the heading of the Model 60-110. The size of the tractor was impressive, measuring 21 feet, 10 inches long, 9 feet, 6 inches wide, and over 10 feet high to the top of the canopy that covered the operator's platform and the engine compartment. The radiator held 116 gallons and the fuel tank 95 gallons!

The Twin City 20-35, such as this 1924 model, was made between 1920 and 1926. In 1926 it and the smaller 12-20 were re-rated and renamed as the 27-44 and 17-28 respectively. In those days, the model number designated drawbar horsepower followed by belt horsepower. This 1924 tractor's four-cylinder engine had a massive 5 1/2x6 3/4-inch bore and stroke that resulted in 641 ci of displacement. It could pull a five-bottom or even a six-bottom plow. Gasoline was its primary fuel, but it was also equipped to heat the manifold sufficiently to keep kerosene vaporized. The red hubcaps were probably not original. *Minnesota Historical Society*

The TC emblem and Twin City name were painted on red surfaces raised slightly higher than the rest of the metal on the 20-35's radiator.

Lubrication was somewhat primitive in the 20-35's day. While an oil pump did force lubrication to the crankshaft, it didn't pump lubricating oil up to the rocker arms. So, several times a day the operator would have to oil the rocker arms from atop the engine.

Twin City 16-30: 1917–1920

Weighing in at a modest 7,800 pounds, the Model 16-30 was the smallest of the Twin City tractors when it was introduced in 1917. Like its big brothers it has kept some of its history well hidden. Some of the engines were outsourced from a firm in Red Wing—presumably Minnesota. Specifications list the engine, from all sources, as a vertical four-cylinder L-head with 589 ci from a 5x7 1/2-inch bore and stroke governed at 650 rpm. The cooling system was of the horizontal tubular type with 154 square feet of cooling surface in the radiator, which had a capacity of 35 gallons. Before the end of production this was changed to an automotive core-type radiator.

It was geared for two speeds forward at 2 and 2 3/4 miles per hour and a reverse at 2 3/4 miles per hour.

One of the tractor's advertised features was that the motor and drivetrain were totally enclosed and dust-proof.

Twin City 12-20: 1919–1926

A first for the tractor industry was the Model 12-20's 16-valve engine. It featured two intake and two exhaust valves per each cylinder. The basic design was an inline vertical four-cylinder with 4 1/4x6-inch bore and stroke governed at 1,000 rpm. The ignition was a high-tension magneto with impulse starter. The cast-iron frame was of the unit construction design.

The transmission allowed two forward speeds of 2.2 and 2.9 miles per hour. In 1924 a new engine was designed for this tractor, and in 1926 the Model 12-20 was re-rated to the Model 17-28 TY. This was the result of Nebraska test number 121, which placed the drawbar horsepower at 22 and the belt horsepower at 30.

What's a bus have to do with farm tractors? In this case, a lot. This is a Twin City Model DW bus. The body was manufactured by the Ecklund Brothers Company of Minneapolis, Minnesota, in 1925. *Minnesota Historical Society*

Twin City 20-35: 1920–1926

This tractor was being developed in 1919 and factory testing was completed in October of that year. Field testing in California was completed late the following year so it is possible that a number of these tractors were marketed in 1920. Evidence that they weren't introduced until 1921 is found in an article published in *Implement & Tractor,* which lists five models in production in 1920 and doesn't include the Model 20-35.

The Model 20-35 was built much the same as the Model 12-20 and carried a 5 1/2x6 3/4-inch bore and stroke four-cylinder engine giving 641-ci displacement. One interesting option was a high-compression head for high-altitude operation. This tractor was re-rated in 1926 and designated the Model 27-44 AT. Actual results from Nebraska test number 122 pegged the drawbar horsepower at 34 and the belt horsepower at 49.

A crucial factor that led MS&M to the eventual merger with the Minneapolis-Moline Power Implement Company was the lack of a tillage tool line.

Recognize that Twin City logo? It's the same that appears on the radiators of Twin City tractors of the same mid-1920s era. This is the business end of what will become a Twin City Model DW bus. *Roger Mohr Collection*

MINNEAPOLIS-MOLINE POWER IMPLEMENT COMPANY

Warren C. MacFarlane was very instrumental in bringing about the merger that formed Minneapolis-Moline Power Implement Company. His introduction to the management team at MS&M was precipitated by the company's financial difficulties in the early 1920s. The postwar recession had sapped the company of cash even though its assets had grown by almost $2,000,000 from 1920 to 1923. MS&M found itself with about $1,181,000 of aging debt that creditors wanted paid immediately.

One of its creditors, a New York bank, wanted MS&M to cease manufacturing tractors and sell the tractor division to International Harvester Company. This and other drastic measures were postponed, and in 1924 tractor sales picked up enough that the company was able to continue stalling creditors for a time. In 1925 Chicago bankers dictated some management aid for the company by sending MacFarlane to become vice president and general manager of MS&M. His mandate was either to make the firm profitable or to liquidate the company.

He made it profitable and the following February the board elected MacFarlane to the presidency. Under his guidance the company strengthened its financial position until by 1928 it could concentrate on expanding the business rather than putting out financial fires.

One of the issues that became apparent to everyone in management was the need to offer a full line of machinery to the farmer, especially tillage tools. It was assumed that the company would eventually manufacture its own line, but for the time being it simply continued to sell the Oliver line of plows.

This all changed in 1928 when management learned that J. I. Case had bought Emerson-Brantingham, Allis-Chalmers entered the implement business in force, and Massey-Harris purchased the J. I. Case Plow Works, Inc. This focused management on the necessity of becoming a full-line company.

Just as MacFarlane sought an answer for the farm equipment division of the company, MIC was in desperate need of financial help. In fact MIC approached MS&M with the proposal that the two companies merge.

It was an ideal marriage from the product line standpoint. The implements of MIC would be a strong complement to the Twin

The Twin Cities KT refers to "Kombination Tractor." It was an early attempt to use a standard tractor for row-crop work, so that the farmer needed just one all-purpose tractor. The restorer calls this 1930 model a "merger" tractor because it was developed by the Minneapolis Steel and Machinery Company, one of three firms that merged in 1929 to form the Minneapolis-Moline Power Implement Company. Nebraska tests said it develops 18 drawbar and 23 belt horsepower, which made it capable of pulling a three-bottom plow. The front-mounted three-row cultivator was designed for a tractor that could straddle a 38-inch row.

This 1934 21-32 FTA is considered by its restorer to be the big sister to the KTA and the predecessor of the MM G model. At Nebraska it developed 21 drawbar horsepower and 32 horsepower at the belt from its gasoline engine.

After the Merger—the Transitional Models

Striking the merger deal and signing the papers were the easy part. What lay ahead for the new firm was much more difficult. The workforce, facilities, and production of the three companies had to be folded into one complementary and cooperative entity. MM's new executives would have to reconcile duplication of personnel, real estate holdings, product lines, and wholesale and retail distribution establishments.

Key personnel were soon in place. J. L. Record, past president of MS&M, was the new chairman of the board, while MacFarlane, president of MS&M, was elected president and CEO of the new firm. Another MS&M executive, vice president George L. Gillette, continued as vice president in charge of sales for the new company.

City tractor line. As the deal neared completion MTM asked to be included as a third party to the consolidation. At the end of seven weeks of negotiations papers were signed in Chicago on April 18, 1929. Total combined assets of the new firm was placed at $24,000,000 with total earnings pegged at approximately $20,000,000.

MIC's Harold B. Dinneen became vice president of production and design at the new corporation. W. C. Rich, secretary, and W. S. Peddie, treasurer, of the MS&M organization filled the same offices in the new firm. N. A. Wiff, vice president of MTM, maintained the same position at the new Minneapolis-Moline Power Implement Company.

Administrative offices were established at the Hopkins plant, while tractor and engine operations were centered at the Minneapolis Lake Street facility. The Moline plant housed

the production of all tillage tools except grain drills. The Hopkins factory became the production site for threshers, combines, corn shellers, hay tools, corn pickers, and all power machinery. Grain drills were produced at St. Louis Park, Minnesota, in the former MIC plant used for the same purpose.

Separate engineering departments were established at each location and became responsible for the design and development of new products for the company.

Distribution of the product line was conducted from eight sales divisions with respective headquarters at Kansas City, Missouri; Dallas, Texas; Omaha, Nebraska; Memphis, Tennessee; Peoria, Illinois; Hopkins, Minnesota; Fargo, North Dakota; and Stockton, California. Plus, strategically located transfer houses were maintained within each division.

Tractors were among the items duplicated in the three companies' product lines. Tillage tools didn't present a big problem since MIC was the only firm that brought these products to the merger.

MS&M had the Twin City line, which included tractors, threshers, industrial engines, structural steel, and a combine ready for production. MTM produced the Great Minneapolis Line consisting of tractors, threshers, combines, shellers, and industrial engines. MIC offered the Flying Dutchman Line of plows, harrows, cultivators, drills, and planters.

The tractors and threshers of both MTM and MS&M had considerable market overlap. The MTM thresher and sheller were more widely known than the Twin City products, so the latter were withdrawn from the line.

Model designations

T	=	tractor
U	=	universal, or tricycle
N	=	single front wheel
S	=	standard (wide) nonadjustable front axle
E	=	wide extendable, or adjustable front axle
U	=	when used by itself in a serial number stands for a power unit only
I	=	industrial
L	=	shuttle tranny in industrials
C	=	cane or hi-crop model
C	=	also stands for propane in the "G" series
X prefix	=	experimental
X suffix	=	military. The exception is the UDLX and the UTX Comfortractor.

Twin City KTA of 1937 mounts a four-cylinder gasoline engine producing Nebraska-verified 19 drawbar and 30 belt horsepower on rubber. This is a bit more than the 24 drawbar and 33 belt pulley horsepower obtained from the more common fuel, distillate. Most farmers started on gasoline and changed to distillate.

A close-up view of the engine and exposed flywheel on a 21-32. It wasn't until this tractor had been upgraded to the GTA with an improved engine that the flywheel was enclosed.

Production of Twin City MTAs, such as this 1935 model, began in 1934. The 283-ci engine provided 35 drawbar horsepower through a four-speed transmission. At the belt it was rated at 33 horsepower. It's the forerunner of the later, highly successful U model. While the red wheels add a nice touch of color, the original paint scheme of these tractors featured gray wheels.

After reviewing its tractor lineup, the new company chose the Twin City line. There was, however, a transitional period when both Twin City and Minneapolis tractors were marketed until the inventory of components for the Minneapolis tractors was exhausted.

Twin City 17-28 TY: 1926-1935

This is a re-rated tractor, previously the Model 12-20, that offered more horsepower to the farmer. The power plant was a vertical four-cylinder 16 valve-in-head design with 340 ci from a bore and stroke of 4 1/4x6 inches. Governed speed was 1,075 rpm, up from the 1,000 rpm on the Model 12-20. An

option on the transmission added a high gear that allows travel of 4.5 mph in high gear. The standard tranny is a 2/1 with two forward speeds of 2.2 and 3 mph. Other options include a PTO, 6, 8, or 12-inch wheel extensions, canopy, and lighting equipment.

During this tractor's heyday, the Midwest Canning Corporation of Rochelle, Illinois, proclaimed that it maintained the "world's largest fleet" of tractors, consisting of 124 TC 17-28 TY machines.

Twin City 17-28 TY Industrial: 1934

Advertised as the "Road Chief," this tractor made the metamorphosis to an industrial

tractor with the same specifications as the agricultural Model 17-28 by adding, as an option, 10x50-inch solid rubber tires. Although we found only one serial number for the industrial, 4300 A, it is almost certain that this was the beginning number and others were produced.

Twin City 27-44 AT: 1926-1935

When the Model 20-35 was re-rated to the Model 27-44 AT in 1926, the high compression heads became standard. Almost all other specifications remained the same as the Model 20-35 with the exception of the carburetor, which was changed from a Holley to a Schebler.

A 1938 model, this is one of the last MTAs made after a nine-year production run. The four-cylinder gasoline engine made by MM had a 4 1/4x5-inch bore and stroke, which generated enough horsepower to make it a three-bottom plow tractor. Although it has turning brakes, it has only a hand clutch. Either a two-row or four-row cultivator could be mounted on the MTA. The red item at the rear is cultivator lifting equipment that could also be used with a planter. The original spoke wheels have been modified to accommodate rubber tires.

Although the Twin City name is still utilized, by 1935 this MTA also sported an accompanying MM logo rather than the previous TC logo. Note the distinctive radiator cap that repeats the MM name.

Twin City 27-44 AT Industrial

Dubbed the "Road King," the industrial version of the Model 27-44 AT also offered the option of solid rubber tires for industrial applications.

Twin City 21-32: 1926-1928

These tractors were first offered with a two-speed Model 17-28 transmission and a 381-ci four-cylinder FE engine governed at 1,000 rpm. The redesigned version became the FT in 1929.

Twin City 21-32 FT: 1929-1934

It was with the Model 21-32 FT that MM began designating experimental tractors with an "X" prefix. Six experimental models of the Model 21-32 FT were made carrying serial numbers X1 through X6.

The FT used the same engine as the Model 21-32 but upped the rpm to 1,075. Engine fuel could be gasoline, kerosene, or distillates thanks to the "Hot Spot" manifold.

The 3/1 transmission gave forward speeds of 2.36, 3.17, and 4.05 mph.

Options available were PTO, lighting equipment with or without a battery, canopy top, industrial wheels with rubber tires, and extension rims.

Twin City 21-32 FTA: 1935-1938

This tractor was almost identical to the previous Model 21-32 tractors, only the FTA used a Type GE engine. The bore on the four-cylinder engine was increased to 4 5/8-inch, while the stroke remained at 6 inches, giving 403-ci displacement. Otherwise the

This JTS was manufactured in 1936, and so shows both the Twin City name and the MM logo on its radiator. It came equipped with spade-style steel wheel lugs, although rubber tires were available as an option.

Produced in 1936 the Twin City Universal JTU row-crop model has a narrow front-end configuration. The standard version was called the JTS. The four-cylinder gasoline engine was built by Waukesha. Bore and stroke are 3 5/8x4 1/2 inches. The JTU was smaller than the MTA or the KTA, and would become the Z model later in 1936.

transmission and options were the same as the FT model. The FTA was only available with standard front axle and weighed 6,080 pounds. This tractor proved to be very popular for threshing and plowing in Western Kansas and other wheat-producing states.

Twin City 21-32 FT Industrial: 1932-1937

Equipped with the 381-ci FE engine, the main difference between the agricultural FT and the industrial versions were wheels and tires, fenders, and an optional spring suspended front axle.

Twin City KT: 1929-1934

This is regarded as the first tractor designed and produced entirely under MM management. The KT designation meant "Kombination Tractor" reflecting the idea that this tractor could do a combination of jobs and chores around the farmstead. It was designed to cultivate three rows of row-crop, straddling the center row.

It was powered by the KE engine, a four-cylinder 283-ci vertical valve-in-head, governed at 1,000 rpm. The 3/1 transmission allowed forward speeds of 2.1 to 4.15 mph. The KT was tested at Nebraska in 1930, yield-

ing 18 horsepower on the drawbar and 25 on the belt.

A KT Orchard Model was also offered from 1929 to 1934. The KT-I was the industrial model, with optional hard rubber tires, which was produced from 1932 to 1935.

Twin City KTA: 1934-1938

Horsepower was increased with this next generation of the KT model. The KEA engine had the same specs but ran at 1,150 instead of 1,000 rpm. Nebraska test number 247, in 1935, placed the drawbar horsepower at 24 and belt horsepower at 33.

Shown in its heyday is the Minneapolis-Moline Implement Plant located at Moline, Illinois. The plant closed down in 1957. In 1929, at the time of the merger, the Moline facility was designated to build all the new company's tillage tools. *Minnesota Historical Society*

Today, nobody knows whether this tractor labeled a "Western Special" was a prototype that was never manufactured or a special order tractor built on a custom basis. It appears to be an industrial version of the "J" series. *Roger Mohr Collection*

This Indiana farmer has hitched his Twin City 21-32 to a three-bottom plow. In addition to plowing, he's also pulling a drag that smooths out the just-turned soil.

Although no separate serial numbers were listed for either an orchard model or an industrial model, it is possible that such variants were produced.

Standard features included individual wheel brakes, dual air cleaner, and oil filter. A 1934 catalog and a 1935 price list both show rubber tires as being available, though they never became standard equipment.

Universal MT: 1930-1934

MM's first row-crop tractor was factory rated for distillate fuel at 19 drawbar and 29 belt horsepower. Nebraska test number 197, conducted in 1931, pegged the maximum drawbar horsepower at 18 and the maximum belt horsepower at 26.

The four-cylinder 283-ci engine could operate on gasoline, kerosene, or distillates thanks to the patented "Hot Spot" manifold. A lighting package was offered as an option, but an electric starter wasn't available. The governed speed of the engine was 1,000 rpm while the 3/1 tranny moved the Universal forward at 2.1, 3.13, or 4.15 mph.

A full bevy of mounted implements was available, including a mounted corn planter, cultivator, lister, middlebreaker, and others.

Universal MTA: 1934-1938

Equipped with MM's 283-ci KEA engine with governed speed of 1,150 rpm, the MTA was Nebraska tested as 24 drawbar and 33 belt horsepower. Seventy octane gasoline was becoming more widely available so an

optional high compression head was offered for those who wished to use the new fuel.

Another option was high speed gears that gave a top road speed of 10 mph. The standard transmission was the 3/1 used in the Model MT.

Universal JT: 1934-1937

Using an engine other than its own seems out of character for MM but that's what they did in the Model JT. The choice was a 196-ci Waukesha, Type JE, operating at 1,275 rpm. Nebraska test number 233, in 1935, gave a horsepower rating of 17 drawbar and 24 belt.

A touted feature of the JE engine was a valve arrangement that located the exhaust valves in the block and the intake valves in the head, a configuration that was supposed

The KTA utilized the same basic 283-ci engine that later became the power plant for the extremely popular Model U tractor. In 1935 the KTA was tested at Nebraska where it produced 24 drawbar and 33 belt horsepower. Note the French and Hecht (F & H) round spoke wheels and owner-installed lights.

This is a scene from the late 1930s with the MTA model belted up to a threshing machine. Notice the power lift for use with a cultivator.

Rolling along on steel wheels some time in the mid-1930s, this MTA pulls a binder cutting grain.

to give superior engine cooling. Perhaps it didn't work as well as planned, since MM Dealer Bulletin D-33 listed a factory package to install an MM Type RE engine on the JT tractor. This conversion package was very popular in the 1940s.

These tractors hustled to work a little faster than their predecessors due to a 5/1 transmission allowing forward speeds of between 2.1 and 12.1 mph.

Rear wheel tread was adjustable from 54 inches to 76 inches and the customer could choose between steel or rubber. A complete line of two- and four-row implements were available for row-crop work.

It is generally accepted that the first 25 JTs, serial numbers 550001-550025 inclusively, were prototypes. A good way to spot these units is by the difference in the radiators. The first prototypes had a flat front on the top radiator tank with no lettering. Production models had "Twin MM City" embossed on the top tank.

In the fall of 1936, a Corn Belt farmer rigs up a way to pull both a plow and a harrow with his new MTA model tractor in order to both turn the soil and smooth it out.

Back in the days before self-propelled combines, this match-up of a Model MT pulling a large Model G Minneapolis-Moline combine was considered close to optimum. This is an example of very early rubber tire conversions using the F & H round spoke wheels.

Birth of the Jeep

The first military vehicle called a "Jeep" was born at Minneapolis-Moline Power Implement Company, and it acquired its name at Camp Ripley, Minnesota.

In 1938 Minneapolis-Moline engineers were well along in experiments that converted a farm tractor to an artillery prime mover. Later in 1940, Adjutant General E. A. Walsh, Commander of the Minnesota National Guard, had the MM vehicles tested in maneuvers at Camp Ripley. The MM-designed model proved unstoppable and was able to do almost anything the Guardsmen asked it to. It reminded the men of the Popeye cartoon character, named Jeep, who knew all the answers and could do anything. As a result of the likeness, the Guardsmen named the MM vehicle the "Jeep."

Almost immediately other manufacturers of military vehicles began using the name "Jeep." In 1942 the House Committee on Military Affairs justly validated MM's claim to the "Jeep" name.

MM went on to design several additional military tractors in cooperation with Army and Navy officials. Some of these models were produced in quantity for the Armed Forces but the major contract for the military "go-anywhere reconnaissance vehicle" went to the Willys-Overland Company and to the Ford Motor Company.

Both an Orchard Model, the JTO, and a Standard Model, the JTS, joined the line from 1936 to 1937. An experimental Orchard JT, carrying serial number X108, is recorded in the MHS serial number list.

LT: 1930

The LT could be called the MM Mystery Tractor. There are serial numbers listed for 10 tractors and we know they had a four-cylinder engine with 4 1/4x5-inch bore and stroke. The MHS serial number list states they were exported to Argentina. It is possible that the LT stood for the "Link Track Tractor" which was a track-laying MM model.

No other information has surfaced about the Model LT.

YT: 1937-1938

From the clutch back the Model YT was very similar to the Model R tractor, but from the clutch forward things were very different. The engine was a two-cylinder Model YE— one-half of a four-cylinder RE engine.

Production, or experimentation, stopped after only 25 tractors were built.

New in 1937, this Model J tractor is being used to pull a double-disc over corn stalk fields in late fall in order to incorporate the stalks into the soil in preparation for next spring's planting.

All standard Z models, such as this ZTS, had flat crown fenders from the day they were introduced in 1937 until they were discontinued in 1947. The standard, identified by the "S" in ZTS, was more commonly seen in the Western states than in the Corn Belt. Early models had 31 belt horsepower and the later models had 36 to 38 horsepower.

PURE PRAIRIE GOLD: MIDRANGE POWER

The new MM company survived the Depression, which began almost before the ink was dry on the corporate papers, and was still able to contribute to the war effort by providing both farm implements and military materiel, despite rationing.

By 1939, at the end of its first decade, MM had designed, tested, and put into production the Model Z and the Model U tractors. The Model R would follow the next year. These were some of the company's most successful tractors and made MM a strong contender in the accelerating market shift toward power farming.

At the end of the company's second decade, stockholders approved a change in the firm's name to the Minneapolis-Moline Company, effective in 1949. By this time the postwar demand for new tractors was in full swing. Tractor production, all brands and models, reached an all-time high in 1948 with 753,623 units produced. Wheel-type accounted for 529,587 units; garden tractors, both riding and push-type, tallied 184,624 units; and track-type units numbered 39,412. About 2 percent, or 15,000 units, were exported to foreign countries. In 1950 the number of tractors on American farms was approaching approximately 4 million.

MM ZTU: 1936-1948

What makes a Model Z a Model Z is the engine. Otherwise it is basically a Model J with a bit longer clutch housing. The new RE engine that debuted on the Model Z had a lot of novel features that were hawked in company advertisements. The engine was a four-cylinder with 185-ci displacement and a 3 5/8x4 1/2-inch bore and stroke. It could be fitted with interchangeable heads specifically for tractor fuel or 70-octane gasoline. Or, the standard "Hot Spot" manifold could be adjusted to let you burn either fuel without changing the heads. For proper combustion and economy, however, it was necessary to change heads for the specific fuel being used.

It was a variable speed engine that would govern between 900 and 2,000 rpm with a standard operating speed of 1,500 rpm. Tested at Nebraska in 1940, test number 352, a ZTU rated 26 drawbar and 31 belt horsepower. The 5/1 transmission gave forward speeds of 2.2 to 14.3 miles per hour.

Quoted in *Farm Implement News* on July 29, 1937, MM Chief Tractor Engineer A. W. Lavers had this to say about the new Model Z's engine: "The 'Z' has an engine as outstanding as the previously developed transmission and rear end (referring to the Model J tractor). For it has literally 140 less motor parts, and it can be serviced from a milk stool with no oil drip in the eyes. In fact, you can put the 'Z' in the parlor and it won't smear the rug. It has no oil pan at all. The crankcase is one solid casting without a gasketed joint below the plane of the shaft."

He continues to explain that a valve-in-head engine design is preferable for burning heavier fuels, and the new engine is a valve-in-head but the "heads" are on the side of the engine and the valves are set horizontal. They are actuated by a rocker arm operating off a camshaft.

Built in 1937, ZTU provided its owner with 35 drawbar horsepower, enough to pull a three-bottom plow. There is probably an interesting story behind the tractor because the air cleaner isn't correct for a 1937 model and the cast-iron front wheels don't fit with the right side location of the air cleaner.

An illustration of wartime shortages is this 1943 ZTU's steering wheel. Because rubber was in such short supply, the tractor was delivered with what Minneapolis-Moline happened to have on hand—in this case a cast-iron steering wheel.

How is an engine serviced from a milk stool? Lavers explains it this way: "Sit down on your stool with a suitable wrench, back off the bolts on the camshaft side of the block and two plates come off. Before you are the connecting rod bearings and the tappets for any needed adjustments.

"Go around to the other side, sit down comfortably, remove those bolts and off comes the spark plug cylinder head cap. And, there are your valves open for grinding."

Rear wheels are adjustable from 54 inches to 84 inches. Rubber or steel was available at the introduction of the Model Z tractor along with automotive-type brakes. When it was first introduced, a starter wasn't available, so it was a "hand-crank-only" vehicle.

First Model ZTUs appeared in 1936 as prototypes that were all gray in color and resembled a Model J tractor more than the later Model Zs. Serial numbers indicate that a total of 37 of the prototypes were produced.

Built in 1943, this ZTX was one of 254 ZTX tractors built for the U.S. military. It was refined for its day, providing an air compressor that ran off the belt pulley, a 10-inch air cylinder at the back, air brakes, and a cab. The tractor was used as a yard tractor and to haul artillery pieces around.

The Model ZTS came into the lineup in 1937, and except for having a standard front axle along with larger fenders and platform, all other specifications were the same as the Model ZTU.

Both the front and rear wheel designs, for both models, were changed early in 1940 from cast-iron centers with demountable rims to one-piece pressed steel centers and rims. This change began on the ZTU with serial number 567555, and on the ZTS at serial number 610685.

At serial number 565135, and after, the air cleaner on the Model ZTU was moved from the left side of the engine to the right

side. On the Model ZTS this air cleaner change began at serial number 610389.

ZTU rear fenders also underwent a couple of changes. First, at serial number 565235, and after, the flat crown fenders were changed to a round crown style. And, beginning at serial number 575713, the round crown fender gave way to the clamshell wheel guard. These fender changes applied to the Model ZTN also.

Sometime in 1946, between serial numbers 577914 and 578013, the Model Z tractors came equipped with distributor ignition, lights, starter, and battery.

Carrying the same engine and specifica-

tion, the Model ZTN was produced from 1940 through 1948 and the Model ZTE had a two-year run from 1947 through 1948.

The industrial version of the Model Z, the Model ZTI, was an early offering beginning in 1936 and lasting through 1942. The ZTI had 24-inch rear rims, straight I-beam front axle, flat angle iron framed fenders, foot throttle, and hand or foot clutch. A spring-mounted front axle was available as an option.

Only 25 copies of the military Model ZTX were made in 1943, the only year of its manufacture. At the core, the military version was a Model Z tractor tweaked out with

Uncle Sam, more specifically the U.S. Air Force, got this 1952 ZASI military tractor. The ZASI and ZM were two very similar but different military tractors. The ZM used the M220-4 engine while the ZASI featured the 206F power plant.

some extra goodies. It was factory equipped with a cab nearly identical to the Model R cab. Other features were air brakes, an air compressor positioned where the belt pulley normally was, foot clutch, foot accelerator, and a drawbar that could be lowered and raised with an air cylinder.

Today, only four of these military Model Zs are known to exist.

MM ZAS, ZAU, ZAE, ZAN: 1949-1953

The Model Z line was upgraded in 1949 with the introduction of the ZAS, ZAU, ZAE, and ZAN. These models featured a new 206-ci engine with a 3 5/8x5-inch bore and stroke operating at 1,500 rpm. Nebraska test number 44

ber 438, performed in 1950 on the Model ZAU burning gasoline, gave drawbar horsepower of 32 and belt horsepower of 36.

Forward speeds fell between 2.4 and 13.1 miles per hour from the 5/1 transmission. Tread width was fixed at 48 inches on the front axle and 54 inches on the rear.

Operator comforts were improved with an air bag cushion seat and adjustable-height steering wheel. The option package introduced a new hydraulic system for raising, lowering, and controlling mounted and pull-behind implements. The Model ZA could also accommodate MM's Quick-On-Quick-Off mounted implements.

Sharing the same specs was the Model ZAU with reversible tricycle front wheels and

rear-wheel adjustable tread width from 54 inches to 88 inches. Production of this tractor stopped in 1952.

The Model ZAE spec sheet reads the same as its stablemates, including adjustable rear tread the same as the Model ZAU. The front axle was adjustable in 4-inch intervals from 56 inches to 84 inches. Optional equipment included the Uni-Matic hydraulic power system. The Model ZAE cost $2,600 retail.

The Model ZAN differed from the other ZA models only in its sporting a single front wheel.

MM ZASI: 1952 only

"Non-conformist" would aptly describe the Model ZASI because it just didn't follow

No, it's not the UDLX Comfortractor in disguise. Instead it's an R Cab model made in 1944. It's virtually the same as an RT, except for its cab. At the time, it was the only tractor that allowed a full line of mounted equipment to fit around the cab.

the rule concerning serial numbers and serial number prefixes. The "I" would usually indicate an Industrial model, which it was, but it was a special build for the military whose models normally carried an "X" suffix.

Although the records show a serial number prefix for these tractors, 046, the serial numbers apparently were never recorded. What we do have are the engine numbers for the 206F-4, which was used exclusively in these tractors. This was a 206-ci-

displacement design around a 3 5/8x5-inch bore and stroke.

Engine serial numbers 05100001–05100515 indicate that 515 units exited the assembly line.

These tractors did have some variants, which included foot clutch, foot throttle, and a shielded ignition specified by the military. In addition, the oil filter was moved from the standard location under the engine to the left side of the engine. A Model RTI

front axle was fitted to these units as well as rear wheels very similar to the RTI models.

Adding just a bit more confusion to the Model ZASI is a Specification Sheet for the tractor, dated June 9, 1951, located in the Minnesota Historical Society archives. It listed the engine as a 206B-4 with a nonadjustable "Hot Spot" manifold, with all other specifications reading the same as the 206F-4.

Under "Tractor" the spec sheet gives these specifications: 11-inch Rockford single dry

The 1949 RTE was one of the first MM tractors to be produced with the flexibility of an adjustable and extendible front axle. The other R model tractor front ends were the standard, single front wheel, and universal narrow front end with two wheels.

plate, spring-loaded, foot clutch; Bendix, two-pedal foot brakes; fabricated "H" section front axle; cast front wheels with demount-able rims; Ross cam and lever steering gear; cast-iron disc rear wheels drilled for adding duals with demountable rims splined to live axle; Pintle hook drawbar adjustable 14 inch-es to 18 inches above ground.

Fitted with 13.00-24 6-ply Roadbuilder tires and a 5/1 transmission, the tractor offered forward speeds from 2.0 to 11.0 miles per hour.

Miscellaneous standard equipment included a 6-volt electrical system, consisting of starter, generator, battery, lights (2 front, 1 rear, 1 dash), ammeter, switches, starter

button mounted on instrument panel, oil and temperature gauges, plus choke, foot accelerator, and hand throttle.

Right: Head-on view illustrates how wide the RTE's front end could be extended out thanks to its adjustable front axle.

Built in 1953 for the military, the RTIM, "I" for Industrial and "M" for Military, saw service with the U.S. Air Force in Korea as early as 1951. Its primary job was pulling trailers. The tractor's industrial heritage is apparent when the original olive drab paint wears thin.

No specific serial numbers were found for this tractor; we suspect they fell within the Model ZAS serial numbers range.

MM ZM: 1953–1954

In 1953 the Model ZM came along, which appears to be basically the Model ZASI with a larger M220-4 engine. Once again this tractor defied the rules when it came to serial numbers. The first year only 17 units were recorded, serial numbers 07600001– 07600017. The beginning serial number for

1954 was 07600018, but there was no ending number and no notation that this was an "only" tractor.

It isn't clear how many Model ZM vehicles were manufactured. The records for serial number prefixes state that 076 is "ZM Military Tractor w/M220-4 Engine."

MM ZBU, ZBE, ZBN: 1953–1955

Carrying the 206G-4 engine, the ZB models came standard equipped to burn regular-grade gasoline with optional equipment

available for tractor fuel and LP gas. Power was listed as 33 drawbar and 37 PTO factory observed horsepower.

Changes that warranted the "B" designation were the same as those that occurred with the UB model tractors, including a raised operator's platform, foot clutch, double disc brakes, 12-volt ignition, and pressure cooling.

Extra, or optional, equipment included regular or live PTO, power lift, quick attachable break-away couplings, adjustable depth

48

Back from the wars are these three tractors built for the military: from left, 1953 RTIM Military, 1943 ZTX Military, and 1952 ZASI Military.

control stop, selective hydraulic depth control, belt pulley, rear wheel weights, front wheel weights, muffler extension, radiator screen, hour meter, and field conversion front axle from Type U to Type E.

MM RTU: 1939–1954

The Model R was the smallest of the MM tractors, but nevertheless a winner. It had the basics of a well-built, long-lived, "farmer's tractor" with a few special wrinkles.

Simplicity was again a feature of this MM-built Type EE engine, hailed as having about 140 fewer parts than a standard design OHV engine. A feature for easy servicing was horizontal valves with a readily accessible cover plate. The Type EE was a vertical four-cylinder with 3 5/8x4-inch bore and stroke giving 165-ci displacement. Governed speed was 1,400 rpm, making the Model RTU capable of 20 drawbar and 23 belt horsepower, according to Nebraska test 341 conducted in 1940.

Eleven years later, in 1951, the Model R was again tested with the same EE engine running at 1,500 rpm instead of the earlier 1,400, and the compression changed from 5.75-1 to 6.1-1. This time Nebraska test number 468, it rated 23 horsepower at the drawbar and 27 on the belt.

Utilizing a 4/1 transmission, the tractor offered forward speeds between 2.4 and 12.3 miles per hour.

In 1953, Minneapolis-Moline designers and engineers worked on this experimental Z model. Note the somewhat different styling from the regular Z. This was the forerunner of the 445 development. *Roger Mohr Collection*

49

The Minneapolis-Moline Lake Street Tractor Plant was thriving when this photograph was taken in 1948. This is the final inspection area. Most of the tractors shown are Z models, the exception being a Model U and RTI in the foreground. It appears that some of the tractors are being prepared for shipment overseas. *Minnesota Historical Society*

Starter and lights were optional on early RTU tractors, while on later models standard equipment included a 6-volt electrical system with starter, generator, battery, instrument panel light, two headlights and a rearview light, and Flote-Ride Seat. Also

available as an option on later models was the three-point "Hitchor" system.

Additional options consisted of hydraulic power lift, 560-rpm PTO, wheel weights, red taillight, muffler extension, and bug screen, plus a low-compression head for

tractor fuels. Another option was a field conversion to adjustable front axle. First-year serial numbers don't specify the type of front axle, noting simply "RT." Those who know these tractors best believe that they were mostly Universal, or tricycle, models, though

An early 1940s Model ZTU is used to pull a two-row corn husker and accompanying wagon somewhere in Illinois.

a small portion of 1939 production is believed to have been standard models. Model RTS production started in 1940 and ran through 1953.

The most impressive design feature of the tractor was the most novel and exciting option: the cab. Very similar to the UDLX cab, the Model R cab was strictly an option. It made the Model RTU the first row-crop tractor available with a "real" cab.

What makes this model even more interesting is a full line of mounted equipment designed to fit around the cab that allowed the tractors to perform most any job on the farm.

The "new" Model R advertising literature appearing in the late 1940s or early 1950s reflected the change in engine rpm and compression ratio. These new models also featured MM's Quick-On-Quick-Off system for mounted implements.

A styling feature that stuck with the Model R throughout its entire production was the famous red grille. There were also some styling changes during its long run. At serial number 404800, and after, the fuel tank was changed. The squared-off tank of the previous design was changed to a rounded tank end that was supported by the instrument panel and tool box.

The flat fenders with angle iron frame gave way to the clamshell style at serial number 0015001156, and after. Beginning with the 1949 models the hood side panel

There's no comparison between one of today's 20-inch 24-row corn planters and this tractor planter of the early 1940s. Yet the Z and the Moline planter with dry fertilizer attachment were many times more efficient than anything of the horse-drawn era.

When it arrived in 1936, the ZTU was the first all-new Z model to be released. It was designed to replace the JTU model tractor. This 1938 unit is cultivating row-crop with a two-row mounted cultivator.

changed from the butterfly wings with three louvers to the more open style on the RTU, RTS, RTN, and RTE models.

MM RTN: 1940–1951

This model's single front wheel, coupled with rear wheels that adjusted to 96 inches, made it ideal for specialty row-crop cultivation.

Two items of interest appear in the serial number list. First, there apparently weren't any Model RTNs produced in 1943, probably due to the war. And, second, except for the first-year production in 1940, the serial numbers had an "N" suffix until sometime in

52

1942, when it was dropped. We found no explanation for this practice.

MM RTE: 1947–1953

Model R tractors produced with an extendable front axle didn't appear until 1947. Other than the front axle, the RTE had the same specifications as the RTU.

MM RTI: 1940–1955

The industrial version of the Model R carried all the same specifications as the agricultural tractors, and the styling changes that occurred to the agricultural tractors applied to the industrial version also. One

production change worth noting began in 1943 with serial number 409308, at which point the front axle was changed from "light" to "heavy" construction.

Perhaps the industrial model was partly responsible for the side hood design change; with an industrial loader mounted on the tractor, the side hoods couldn't be opened and many operators simply chose to leave these off, giving the tractor an unfinished appearance.

MM RTI-M: 1953 only

According to the serial number prefix record list, the military placed order number ED-DE 5220 for 200 of these tractors. Actual

The lady is driving an MM experimental tractor. It was sent in 1943 to a Prophetstown, Illinois, plow experimental farm. Carrying an R engine, the tractor has square back axles, plus a most unusual hood that's rounded around the headlights. *Roger Mohr Collection*

serial numbers indicate that 249 were produced. What became of the extra 49 isn't known, but they may have been sold as industrial tractors.

What we do know about earlier Model RTI industrial tractors that MM produced for the military is that the military specified pneumatic tires, gasoline-driven engines, and 3,000–3,700 pounds drawbar pull. A few of these military tractors were equipped with an HK hydraulic system.

MM RT Mail Carrier Special: 1939–1940

We know they existed and we know they had to be marvelous for getting the mail through. What we don't know is how many were made, as no specific serial numbers appear to have been assigned to the Mail Carrier Special. Even the production dates are uncertain but we suggest the above as being most likely.

These machines used the EE engine and 4/1 transmission for a top speed of 19 miles per hour. Flat front fenders with guard rails extending to the rear wheels made lots of room for extra mail sacks that wouldn't fit into the cab.

It had to be one of the most dependable and comfortable ways to deliver mail over rural mail routes.

From this angle, the 1937 Z looks even more powerful than it is while pulling a moldboard plow socked in at least 8 inches deep.

Another Minneapolis-Moline First

MM was the first manufacturer to offer a production tractor designed to use LP gas fuel. The first of these tractors were designated as butane models. Butane and propane are closely related liquefied petroleum gasses.

Minneapolis-Moline Sales Letter #267, dated December 11, 1940, and sent to domestic and Canada trade territories, announced the introduction of butane equipment.

> This equipment has been approved. It consists of Butane fuel tank, carburetor, regulator, filter, manifolding, cylinder head, rotary gauge, valves and special piping and fittings. All special and optional equipment we now list for UTS and UTU tractors will fit on the Butane equipped machine without changes, except the electric starting and lighting equipment. At a later date we will announce electric starting and lighting equipment for use on Butane equipped tractors. Butane equipment will not be available for application to tractors in the field or branches. Field changeovers may be made available in the future if sufficient demand for the equipment develops.
>
> Butane equipment will show a 7% increase in horse power over 70 Octane gasoline. Except for this increase in horse power, specifications remain the same for both Butane or regular equipped tractors.
>
> Tentatively we will have Butane equipped machines available for shipment from factory about April 1st, 1941.

It is possible to burn either butane, propane, or a mixture of the two, in the MM tractors without any change in equipment.

There appears to be some confusion about when the first Butane tractors were manufactured. The August 1998 issue of the *Corresponder* states on page 17 that the first LP gas unit was a 1940 Model. However, MHS serial numbers list the first-production tractors as manufactured in 1941. These Model UTS tractors would bear serial numbers 315451–315500. This would seem to be consistent with the above company letter anticipating first delivery in April 1941.

MM has been recognized as a pioneer in the design of tractors and power units using Liquefied Petroleum Gas (LP gas) for agricultural work. LP gas tractors and power units, released by the company beginning in 1941, were among the earliest of their kind. In 1949 the Model U LP was the first factory-designed tractor to be tested at the Nebraska Testing Laboratory using LP gas as a fuel.

"Visibility is just great out of the cab," says a restorer who's used an RTU like this 1939 model equipped with a cab. This cab could be installed on any R model tractor. Its price tag was $165.

Celery harvesting was a back-breaking job, even with a new R model tractor assisting. The tractor was probably a late 1940 model, because only R tractors of that vintage had rounded fuel tank and solid center rear wheels. Since they're mounted backward, it's a pretty good bet that the tractor's main task was cultivating. It is equipped with hydraulic cultivator lift roll shaft and cultivator mounts.

During harvest time in the 1940s, this new RTU model is powering an equally new Harvestor combine through a field of small grain. The "69" refers to the cutter bar width, which is 3 inches shy of 6 feet!

Pick a pair—two RTU tractors in the harvest field are pulling the first Moline Harvestor "69" combines. The width of the cutter bar was 69 inches. Note the early protective shade-roll bar on the following tractor.

Oh, my, but aren't we glad somebody invented the baler? A farm wife drives the R model tractor while two men try to keep up with the hay elevated and dumped onto the trailer by the Minneapolis-Moline loader.

Complete with rifle boot, this 1951 RTI was built for the military. The specifications called for "Tractor, wheel type, pneumatic tires, gasoline engine driven, 3,000 to 3,700 pounds drawbar pull, size 3." *Roger Mohr Collection*

The UTU, in production from 1939 through 1955, saw 5,383 units manufactured in its peak year. This 1952 UTU has 39 drawbar horsepower and 44 belt horsepower.

HIGH-POWERED PRAIRIE GOLD

The Model Z and Model R were the small tractors in MM's line, providing good service for farm tasks requiring small or medium power. Bigger jobs and bigger farms required more muscle so farmers could maximize the benefits and efficiency of power farming. MM met its customers' needs for higher horsepower with its Model U and Model G tractors.

MM UT: 1936–1937

As early as 1936, MM was building standard model prototypes of what would become the UTS. Serial numbers indicate that 25 of these tractors were built for field testing in 1936 and 1937. They used the KEC engine of 283 ci with a 4 1/4 x5-inch bore and stroke. Although the transmission cover would suggest a five-speed, it was really only a three-speed with gearing very similar to the KTA. Also there are many minor details in the castings that vary from the production Model UTS.

MM UDLX: 1938

Two production runs of this "Comfortractor" took place in 1938. Early in the year 25 units, serial numbers 310001–310025, were made in which the cab was an option. The serial number I.D. plate on many, if not all, of these tractors is stamped UTX along with the serial number. Those produced without the cab were also called the UOPN, for open tractor.

The UTX designation is a departure from the regular model designation where the X suffix denotes a military vehicle.

Later in 1938 a production run of 125, serial numbers 310501–310625, was made and on these vehicles the cab was standard equipment. Cabs were not fabricated at the MM facility but were outsourced from another manufacturer.

Power for the UDLX came from MM's KED four-cylinder 283-ci design with 4 1/4x5-inch bore and stroke. The governed speed was normally 1,275 rpm, but automatically changed to 1,785 rpm when shifted into fifth gear.

The UDLX transmission is unique to farm tractors, allowing speeds of up to 40 miles per hour. The idea was to use the tractor for fieldwork and also as an automobile, so you could zip to town for shopping or for Saturday night entertainment.

Special features of the transmission include helical cut gears on third and fourth, which reduce the noise level inside the cab as well as providing on-the-go-shifting between these gears. Also, the second lever on the tranny housing isn't a true overdrive but a countershaft throw-out that disengages all gearing inside the transmission except a straight through shaft for fifth gear. This arrangement reduces friction drag of the other gears, which now weren't running in heavy transmission grease, thus increasing road speed.

Additional features that made the Comfortractor a truly "Deluxe" tractor included safety glass, Philco radio, horn, ashtray, cigar lighter, heater, rearview mirror, clock, windshield defroster, speedometer, windshield wipers, ammeter, oil and temperature gauge, starter, headlights, taillights, and dash lights.

Designed to be a car as well as a tractor, the UDLX Comfortractor was the first assembly-line cab tractor ever built. It could pull a three-bottom plow all day long, and then take the farmer's wife to town at road speeds of up to 40 mph. Its comforts included a radio, hot water heater, cigarette lighter, ashtray, and mirror with a clock. The UDLX was never trucked from one dealership to another. Instead, they were driven by MM blockmen or managers. This particular 1938 UDLX is one of 150 ever built.

The electrical system was 6-volt and the UDLX and the U Standard used the same front axle design.

The UDLX was very advanced for its time and was heavily advertised by MM. Sadly it proved too pricey for farmers to buy. When this became evident to the company, it made an effort to sell them as a UDLX Industrial Model beginning in about 1940. This move met with some success as several cities purchased them equipped with snowplows for street snow removal.

MM UTS: 1938–1957

If the UDLX was a little ahead of its time, the UTS was right on time and several versions of the model were eventually produced.

These machines had a long run and became one of MM's most successful tractors.

KEC and KEF were the engine type designations used in the early Model U tractors. Sometime in early 1940 the switch was made from the KEC to the KEF engines for production Model Us.

These engines had 283-ci displacement from a 4 1/4x5-inch bore and stroke operating at a governed speed of 1,275 rpm.

In 1938 the same tractor, Model UTS serial number 310305, was tested twice, once from October 24 to November 16 and again November 21 to 25. Horsepower rating on the first test, Nebraska test 310, using gasoline, produced 39 horsepower on the drawbar and 42 on the belt. The second test,

Nebraska test 311, yielded 33 drawbar and 36 belt horsepower on distillates. Same tractor, same engine, but different results on different fuels.

Customers could choose from two engine heads: a high-compression version at 5.33 to 1, or a low-compression type at 4.3 to 1. Beginning with the Model Z, and following with the Model U and Model R, MM introduced the famous Visionlined tractors.

In mid-1947 the company changed the engine designation to 283A-4. The 283A-4 had the same bore and stoke and the same displacement. One main difference between the engines was that the KEF and KEC were solid-block designs, while the 283A-4 was a "split block," meaning that the cylinders

Here's a trio of tractors that will work and work and work. All variations of the basic U model, they are from the left, a UTU, a UTI, and a UTS.

were cast in pairs. This feature was a hallmark of MM engines dating back to the Twin City era. In fact, the Model KT, Model KTA, Model MT, Model MTA, and early Model U units were the only MM tractors that utilized MM-built engines that weren't cast in pairs. This included the KEC, KEF, KED, KE, and KEA power plants. The Waukesha JT engine was also a solid-block design.

The KEC and KEF engines used in the early Model U tractors had the same specs with the difference being in the crankshaft, rod, and main bearings. The KEC used insert babbitt bearings while the KEF changed to precession insert bearings.

The change from the KEF to the 283A-4 engine occurred at serial number 334001 and after. The 283A-4 had a distributor ignition instead of the KEF's magneto. This change allowed the installation of an engine-driven

hydraulic pump located on the left side of the engine. At this same time, with serial number 334001, the gear ratio was changed to the 5/1 transmission, resulting in a faster reverse and a slower road gear—roughly 15 miles per hour in road gear.

For the first four years, 1938–1941 inclusive, the MM tractors featured the famous "red face" or "red grille" styling, but with the 1942 models the tractors were totally restyled; the red grille was changed to the bar grille, which was painted the same Prairie Gold as the rest of the tractor. During World War II, steering wheels on the Model U tractors, and some other models, were changed to a five-spoke cast-iron design due to the shortage of rubber.

Tractor serial number plates were located on the top right side of the transmission case and a separate serial number was assigned to,

and placed on, the engines. Tractor production records corresponded to the I.D. plate on the transmission. This requires some interesting, and diligent, interpretation of the serial numbers during Model UTU production.

According to records, a transmission bundle No. 2819x containing 250 transmissions, serial numbers 328501–328750, was shipped to the English firm, Sale-Tilney, in 1946. In 1948, 50 more transmissions, serial numbers 338054–338103, were shipped to England but were later returned to the Lake Street facility and renumbered to serial numbers 0114900001–0114900050. Again in 1948 a second bundle of transmissions, this time 500, was sent to Sale-Tilney. There is no record that these were returned.

According to these numbers, at least 750 transmissions were delivered to Sale-Tilney and used in English tractor production. It is

The KTA evolved into the UTS, with the "S" indicating the Standard version, which preceded the "UT" Universal Tractor. It utilized the same basic engine as the KTA.

unclear just what English-built models these transmissions were used in but it was most likely the UDS, UDI, and UDM. In all probability some of these found their way to South Africa and perhaps other countries.

In 1945, beginning with serial number 323172, the UTS fenders were changed from the large full crown-type to the smaller clamshell design. In 1955 another fender change took place at serial number 01213626, and after, in which the clamshell fender gave way to a larger full cover design.

One year later, in 1956, at serial number 01214126, the Model UTS became the Model UTS Special. The biggest change was the redesign of the radiator and grille to allow room for optional power steering components.

MM was the first tractor manufacturer to offer LP gas as a fuel option on production farm tractors. Beginning in 1941 all versions

of the Model U production tractors could be purchased as "LP gas burners."

A special application of the Model UTS that carried its own serial numbers was the grader conversions. These tractors were stock UTS models fitted with a components package that converted them to road graders. Serial numbers reflect that 100 of these were produced from 1950 to 1951.

Yet another version of the Model UTS was the UTSD-M Diesel, destined to be shipped "knocked down" (partly disassembled) to Turkey from 1954 through 1958. Some experts believe that most of these tractors never made it to Turkey, as many have turned up in the United States and Canada. One way to spot these tractors is the German Bosch injector pumps. Except for these tractors, the injector pumps on the Model UTS Diesel were American-made Bosch products.

MM UTU: 1939–1955

Added to the line in 1939, this row-crop version of the Model U was another best-seller for the company. Basically the same tractor as the Standard Model U, this tricycle model did have some small differences. Like the standard model, sometime in early 1940, the KEC engine was replaced with the KEF engine. Also, starting at serial number 334001, the KEF was replaced with the 283A-4 version of the 283-ci MM-built engine. Another specification change was in the final drive of the row-crop model. This kept the road speed within an acceptable safety range for the slightly more unstable tricycle tractor.

A fender styling change occurred at serial number 321150, and after, when the large full crown fenders were no longer standard production on the Model UTU. These were replaced by the smaller clamshell design.

A rather unique tractor is this 1955 UB Special LP gas model. According to Nebraska tests, it provided 44 horsepower at the drawbar and 50 horsepower at the belt. Although the UB Special had a foot clutch, the operator could stop forward travel by pulling a hand lever. This effectively provided live PTO. Power steering was optional. "The UB Special is just an awfully nice tractor," its restorer observes.

During Model UTU production in 1947, tractors with serial numbers 331626–331652 were equipped with distributor ignitions and hydraulic lifts. These were probably experimental tractors.

Diesel versions of the row-crop Model U appeared in 1952 and 1953 as the UDU Diesel. Only one tractor was serial numbered in 1952 and 29 more in 1953. These 30 units were almost certainly prototypes. They used the D283-4 engine and the 5/1 transmission. Nebraska test number 319, in 1939, established that the UTU had 36 drawbar and 42 belt horsepower.

MM UTC (UTN, UTE): 1945–1955

Cane, or Hi-crop, versions of the Model U started with the 283-ci KEF engine until serial number 336001, when it was replaced

by the 283A-4 sometime during 1947. The Model UTC came with a 6-volt electrical system until in 1954, serial number 08800001, at which time the 12-volt system became standard equipment.

Early optional equipment included starter and generator, lights, PTO, belt pulley, power lift, and wheel weights.

There is evidence in the MHS serial number list that some Model UTCs were converted to Model UTILs, or vice versa.

The transmission case on the industrial models and the cane models was identical, being drilled and machined with an extra axle flange for added strength. The MHS serial number list indicates that a shuttle transmission was used on a small number of cane models. The serial number list seems to indicate that the shuttle transmission models

included serial numbers 328296–328300 and serial number 328328.

From 1950 through 1952, the Model UTN was offered as part of the Model U line-up. The same specs applied to the Model UTN as to other models of the U tractor. Of course the N designated a single front wheel.

In 1951 through 1954, the Model UTE was produced. Again the basic tractor remained the same as the Model U but the front axle was a wide, adjustable tread.

Next Page: The face-off: A 1955 UB Special LP gas is at left and a 1952 UTU is at right. The UB Special LP gas version was offered only in that year. It delivered 44 horsepower at the drawbar from a four-cylinder MM-built Type 283C-4 engine.

Foreign-built MM tractors

Overseas production wasn't a large segment of MM's total operation, but is an interesting aspect of the company's business. Minneapolis-Moline had production facilities in both France and England.

Mathis-Moline—France: 1949–1952

The Mathis-Moline tractors were built under license in France. MM probably supplied the drawings and specifications, but the casting was done in a French facility. "Made in France" was cast into the parts along with the same part number as American castings. All bolts and nuts are metric.

These French tractors were inspired by the Model R and they were produced in Row-Crop, Standard, and Vineyard models. The Mathis-Moline Vineyard was designated the Model VRTE with an EE engine. No MM Vineyard model was made in the United States. The "V" designated Vineyard and "E" denoted a wide adjustable front axle. These are very narrow tractors designed to work between the rows of a vineyard.

French production reached a total of 338 tractors–168 in 1949, 115 in 1950, 44 in 1951, and 11 in 1952.

UDS and UDM—England

We didn't find a great deal of information on these tractors, but they were built in England and used American-made transmissions. These vehicles were powered by either an English-built Dorman or Meadows engine.

Basically they resembled a Model U tractor with a red grill. The rest of the tin work, although somewhat similar in appearance, was definitely different. A 575-rpm PTO was standard equipment as well as a detachable split-type belt pulley. The front tires were 7.50x18 inches, and the rear tires, 12.75x32 inches, mounted on cast-iron centers. Wheel weights and liquid ballast could be used.

Optional, or extra, equipment included rear winch, electric lighting, and steel wheels with road bands.

Both engine versions, Meadows (UDM) and Dorman (UDS), were diesel models rated 65 and 46 brake horsepower, respectively. The Meadows specifications read like this: type—diesel 4 DC 420 (cold starting), cylinders—4, firing order—1, 3, 4, 2, bore and stroke—130x130 mm, normal governed speed (full load)—1,275 rpm.

Dorman specifications were as follows: type—diesel 4 DWD (cold starting), cylinders—4, firing order—1, 3, 4, 2, bore and stroke—115x 130 mm, normal governed speed (full load)—1,275 rpm.

If the Dorman or Meadows engine didn't fit the customer's needs or wants, the American-built Model U could also be fitted with a Perkins diesel engine conversion package.

MM UTS Diesel: 1952–1956

Serial numbers 05000001–05000018 fell in the category of experimental or prototype diesel tractors. These were built in 1952. Real production of the UTS Diesel model didn't seem to get under way until 1954 according to serial number records. This tractor became the "Special" model in 1956, which meant it had the redesigned radiator and grille to allow for power steering if desired.

The diesel model used the D283-4 engine with the same 283 ci as the gasoline and LP gas models. The diesel was governed at 1,300 rpm and was rated at 40 drawbar and 45 belt, or PTO, horsepower. Options were PTO, hydraulic lift, and a live PTO, which could be either factory or field installed. A hand clutch activated MM's 5/1 transmission.

MM UBU: 1953–1955

A raised operator's platform, foot clutch, and disc brakes were just three of the upgrades of the Model U that appeared with the Model UB tractors. Operator comfort

and conveniences were beginning to receive more attention as farmers demonstrated that they were willing to pay for some creature comforts on their machinery.

With the introduction of the Model UB, a 12-volt electrical system became standard on the entire Model U series.

Gasoline, tractor fuel, and LP gas fuels were all compatible, and available, with the 283B-4 engine. Drawbar horsepower respectively for these fuels was 42, 37, and 44.

The Model UBE and Model UBN were also produced from 1953 through 1955 as the same tractor with a different front axle package.

Joining the line in 1954, and available through 1955, was the UBU Diesel and the UBE Diesel. They carried the 283-ci D283-4 engine governed at 1,300 rpm and delivered 40 drawbar and 45 PTO horsepower. The standard 5/1 transmission allowed forward speeds of 2.8 to 15.7 miles per hour. In 1954 only, 48 copies of the Model UBN Diesel were produced.

MM UB Special: 1955 only

As mentioned, the Special designation reflected a design change in the grille and radiator to allow for the option of power steering. At this time the "B" tractors also introduced interchangeable front-wheel equipment designed with a key lock configuration that allowed any of the front axles, U, E, or N, to be mounted to these tractors.

The Special tractors, fitted with the 283C-4 engine, gave the customer the choice of using tractor fuel, gasoline, or LP gas. Burning tractor fuel netted 37 horsepower at the drawbar, gasoline 48, and LP gas 44.

The UB Special Diesel was produced from 1955 through 1957 using the D283-4 engine that yielded 40 drawbar and 45 PTO horsepower. MM's diesel engines had two oil rings, while the gasoline and LP gas engine had only one.

A 12-volt electrical system with starter and lights were standard equipment, and live PTO and hydraulics were options.

A beefier version with smaller fenders was the UTI, with the "I" standing for Industrial. This 1938 UTI mounts an extremely heavy front axle, what the company termed a "10,000-pound front axle." It utilizes 8.50x20 or 9.00x20 truck wheels and rims at the front. The tractor was often seen running a Lull industrial front-end loader.

MM UTI: 1940–1956

The Industrial version of the Model U was rolled out in 1940 using the same KEF engine as the agricultural tractor and a 5/1 transmission that was, depending on tire size, perhaps a bit slower than the agricultural tractors, capable of only 14 miles per hour in high gear. A few extra options were available on the industrial models that weren't offered on the agricultural versions. These included a power box with two PTO shafts, power lift, and air compressor. Regular options were electric starter, generator, lights, belt pulley, and rear PTO. A heavy-duty front axle was added to the options list in 1941 and became standard equipment in 1945.

Starting at serial number 334001, the 283A-4 engine replaced the KEF. Just like

the agricultural line, beginning in 1942 the red grille was changed to the bar grille.

In 1945 the rear fenders were changed from the flat metal design with angle iron frame to clamshell wheel guards identical to the agricultural tractors. In 1953 the 12-volt electrical system replaced the previous 6-volt system.

In 1956 there were six copies of the UTID manufactured. The only difference was the D283-4 diesel engine instead of the 283A-4 gas power plant.

MM UTIL: 1948–1957

This Industrial model introduced the shuttle transmission, referred to as either the 5/1 with reverse shuttle or the 6/6 shuttle. Either way it gave six forward and six reverse speeds. Forward ranged from 2.2 to

14.5 miles per hour and reverse from 1.8 to 12.6 miles per hour.

Like the later UTI models, it used the 283A-4 engine capable of burning tractor fuel, gasoline, or LP gas. In 1953 these tractors also switched to the 12-volt electrical system.

Sometime about 1950, the company began calling the industrial line the Industrial Wheelers instead of Industrial Tractors.

Painted olive drab and headed for military service, the UTIL-M was produced in 1953 only. This tractor had the standard agricultural front axle and hydraulic brakes. Two copies were produced with 12-volt electrical systems and a separate set of serial numbers, while the remaining 355 were manufactured with 6-volt systems and their own set of serial numbers.

Although not exactly beautiful, the restorer may be somewhat critical when he comments that his 1950 UG Motograder American 900 is "Ugly." Basically this is a U tractor with its front wheels removed and the front grader wheels extended forward for better leveling work. American Road Equipment Company, Omaha, Nebraska, built the grader.

This tractor started life as a 1954 UTS. After the front wheels were removed, a grader was mounted on the front end that utilizes the tractor's hydraulic system. The combination of standard power steering and excellent articulation allows for extremely short turns. The triple-threat unit mounts a grader blade, scarifier, and bulldozer blade. The manufacturer of this conversion isn't known but the unit is different from the Motograder made by the American Road Equipment Company.

The UTIL-D appeared in 1953 and lasted until 1959. It was introduced with the 12-volt electrical system and used the D283-4 valve-in-head diesel engine with the Lanova combustion system.

Another semi-rare industrial model is the UMIL with 42 copies produced in 1953 only. These were also military units painted olive drab and were basically a Model UTIL with a GTB 340B-4 engine, radiator, and front axle.

MM GT: 1938–1941

This tractor was nearly identical to the Model FTA 21-32 with the most significant difference being the tin work and paint color; the Model GT came with MM's own GE power plant of 403 ci with a 4 5/8x6-inch bore and stroke. When introduced it was governed at 1,075 rpm and tested at Nebraska with 47 drawbar and 55 belt horsepower.

The 21-32 begot the GT which in turn begot this 1944 GTA. It utilizes a 403-ci engine producing 60 horsepower mated to a four-speed transmission. The GTA was an important milestone, because it was the first of a long line of what became known as "Big, ol' tractors."

This was test number 317 conducted in May of 1939.

Fitted with a 4/1 transmission, forward speeds ranged from 2.7 to 9.6 miles per hour. Only the standard front axle was available. Low-compression heads for tractor fuel were an option. At this stage of the Model GT's life, it came with a Fairbanks-Morse FM magneto with flange-mounted impulse coupling. Six-volt starting and lighting equipment was available as an option.

The industrial version, the Model GTI, shared the same type engine and also had a 4/1 transmission. Front and rear wheels were cast-iron discs with demountable rims. Rear wheels were drilled for wheel weights or duals. Fenders were the flat style reinforced with angle iron edging.

A long list of options included electric starter and lights, belt pulley, rear-end PTO, front-end PTO for grader units, power box

for grader controls, spring-mounted front axle, hydraulic pump, air compressor for tire inflation, and "Hot Spot" manifold for tractor fuel. It could be ordered with a downdraft exhaust system.

Red grille, cast frame, and exposed flywheel are good tip-offs that it's a Model GT.

MM GTA: 1942–1947

Upgrades that made the Model GT into a Model GTA involved both styling and mechanicals. The engine was changed from the Type GE to the Type LE. The "red face" was gone: it was the same grille style only painted yellow, and the exposed flywheel was now enclosed. No longer was the frame cast but was now fabricated of channel iron.

Engine and transmission specs remained the same as the Model GT during its early production. Around 1943 company brochures begin to list the rpm as 1,100, up

just 25 rpm from the previous governed speed. Otherwise the drivetrain remained the same.

MM GTA-I Industrial: 1946

Again production years and serial numbers remain somewhat of a mystery. The serial number list from the MHS identifies this model as being made in 1946 only. The difficulty is that company *Bulletin No. T-701* dated February 1945, and *Bulletin No. T-701* dated August 16, 1943, both give engine and tractor specifications for GTA Standard Industrial Tractor with the Type LE engine. So it's very likely that some of Model GTA industrial versions were made before 1946.

Neither of the above sheets lists LP gas as a fuel option; however, there are serial numbers for six LP gas GTA Industrial tractors produced in 1946.

Although it carries the correct decals for a G model, the restorer considers this 1951 model to be a GTB since it has clamshell fenders. It has 58 belt horsepower. Over the years the restorer remembers hitching a number of different G tractors to four-bottom and five-bottom plows, a couple of which ran on propane.

MM GTB: 1947–1954

This next revision of the Model GT tractor used the 403A-4 engine and a 5/1 transmission that squeezed out just a few more horses than the Model GTA.

Nebraska test number 437, conducted in 1950, said it was capable of 49 horsepower on the drawbar and 58 at the belt. Just one copy of the Model GTB Diesel was made in 1953 followed by 849 tractors in 1954. The diesel version used the D425-6 MM-built engine.

A 12-volt system was standard equipment while PTO, wheel weights, hydraulics, and rice tires fell in the options category.

There doesn't seem to be a Model GTB Industrial per se, but *MM Bulletin No. 2004* includes a picture and specifications for "MM Model GTB for drawbar application on

industrial jobs." The specs are pretty much those of the GTB agricultural tractor.

Model Gs were available in LP gas starting in 1950.

The *MM Engine Serial Numbers Numerical Identification* lists the 340-4 engine in GTB tractors from 1951 to 1953 and also the 403-A and 403C-4 in GTB tractors from 1947 to 1962.

MM GTC: 1951–1953

Here again MM departed from its standard suffix designation. In this case the "C" suffix doesn't mean Cane Model but rather LP gas. Hence this version of the Model GT was offered in LP gas only.

The engine is Type 340-4, which was apparently used only in this tractor. Engine serial numbers total 1,107 units and tractor

serial numbers total 1,101, indicating that this was the only production machine to have used this particular engine.

MM GB: 1955–1959

In its day this was the top end for horsepower in the MM lineup. These were four- and five-plow tractors with lots of lugging power from MM's 403-ci four-cylinder engine. In 1955, Nebraska test number 547, the gasoline model was rated for 59 and 65 horsepower at the drawbar and belt, respectively.

Also in 1955, Nebraska test number 545, the LP gas version yielded 62 drawbar and 70 belt horsepower.

The 5/1 tranny gave forward speeds of 2.7 to 14.7 miles per hour. A 12-volt ignition system with starter, generator, battery, headlights, rearview light, plus a belt pulley

Coming off the assembly line in 1953, this GTC is powered by LP gas fuel. Its engine has a displacement of 340 ci. The GTC was the only MM tractor that used the Type 340-4 MM-built engine.

were all standard equipment. Options, or extra equipment, available were Uni-Matic Power hydraulic system for pull-behind implements, hydraulic jack, 495-rpm PTO, red taillight, bug screen, and muffler with spark arrester.

The GB weighed in at 6,600 pounds without added weights, which were available as an option.

MM GB-D Diesel: 1955–1959

By the time the Model G tractors were introduced, diesel fuel was becoming increasingly popular with farmers and MM's diesel version of the Model GB gave them that fuel option. The engine was a D425-6 six-cylinder with 4 1/4x5-inch bore and stroke governed at 1,300 rpm. Nebraska test 568, in 1955, said it produced 55 drawbar and 62 belt horsepower.

This engine used the Lanova-type combustion system. Fitted with the usual 5/1 transmission, it gave forward speeds of 2.7–14.7 miles per hour.

Just like the gasoline and LP gas models, this tractor was also made for Massey-Ferguson. From the radiator back, the MF-95 was vintage MM Model GB. The radiator and grille work were changed for the Massey tractors and, of course, the colors were consistent

This GB model was manufactured in 1957. The tractor's LP gas engine was of 403-cubic inch size. Nebraska tests put the LP gas version of the GB at 62 drawbar and 70 belt horsepower.

with Massey-Ferguson paint. The MF-95 was marketed in direct competition with the MM Model GB.

The MF-95 Diesel production amounted to 1,100 copies for Massey-Ferguson. MM's production under the Model GB-D badge was 2,790 tractors.

In retrospect, selling this tractor to Massey-Ferguson probably wasn't a wise decision, but someone in the big office felt it was the right thing to do.

MM UTX: 1939–1941

Only six of these experimental military tractors are recorded in the serial number list. Two different gasoline engines were used in these military vehicles. The four-cylinder version carried the MM-built KEF engine with 283-ci displacement. Those of the six-cylinder design had the MM-built CEA 425-ci version with 4 1/4x5-inch bore and stroke. The governed engine speed was 1,300 rpm producing 71 PTO horsepower.

This 1939 UTU shared a similar 283-ci engine with the MTA, which it replaced in the MM stable of tractors. Note the cast center front wheels, which were used on the early UTUs.

The Model UTX underwent a progression of changes from a four-cylinder two-wheel drive, much like an open Comfortractor, to an open four-wheel drive with the six-cylinder engine. Then the vehicle driver and passenger area was enclosed on the four-wheel-drive six-cylinder, followed by an enclosed six-cylinder with dual wheels. The transmission on all versions was MM's usual 5/1.

Apart from these facts, information is almost nonexistent. A handwritten note gives us a clue about tractor X158. It was built October 29, 1941, and had engine serial number 547178, which is a KEF engine manufactured in 1941, making it the same 283-ci engine used in some Model U tractors.

One of these experimental models, serial number X170, is still around today residing in a restorer's collection.

MM NTX: 1942–1944

Even though more of these military tractors were built, it doesn't give out its secrets any more freely than the Model UTX.

The engine was MM's 206-ci four-cylinder of the same basic design as the engine used in the Model Z tractor, but for the Model NTX the engine had hydraulic valve lifters.

The Model NTX was designed as an aircraft towing tractor and therefore had four-wheel drive and the same 5/1 transmission as the Model Z tractor, but fitted with a two-speed underdrive.

As a note of interest, both the Twin City 25-45s, with a crossmount engine, and the first Model UTX built in 1942, used the beginning serial number of 2501. It's interesting

One of Minneapolis-Moline's experimental tractors in 1947 was this GTB set up to run on butane. MM pioneered the use of LP gas in farm tractor engines. *Roger Mohr Collection*

but probably doesn't mean anything except that there was a Twin City list and an MM list of serial numbers.

MM GTX: 1942–1944

An apt description of the Model GTX is a "big" six-cylinder, six-wheel, six-wheel-drive 10-man-crew prime mover—this is an impressive vehicle. Wheelbase is 107 inches, overall length 202 inches, and it measures 115 inches high with the canvas top and windshield. Its rated payload is three tons, it has an estimated drawbar pull of 13,500 pounds, and weighs 19,300 pounds. Standard equipment was a Gar Wood model 3M front winch as well as Wagner hydraulic brakes activated by a Westinghouse air compressor.

As big as it was, the GTX moved pretty fast, with a top speed of 30.6 miles per hour. The three-speed tranny included a planetary-type underdrive between the engine and transmission, effectively giving six forward speeds. At 1,000 rpm in first gear, on the low side, it traveled 1.8 miles per hour.

Standard accessories included tachometer, speedometer, windshield wiper, canvas top and side curtains, complete blackout lighting, two regular headlights and one tail-light, two 6-volt batteries for lighting and ignition, and 12-volt starting.

A specification sheet dated December 18, 1942, lists the six-cylinder engine as a Type HEA, 605 ci with 4 5/8x6-inch bore and stroke governed at 1,800 rpm. All this information is a bit confusing because an HEA engine doesn't show up on any of the engine serial number lists. In fact, it doesn't appear that MM ever made a 605-ci engine for tractors. The only 605-ci engine listed, Type HE, is for a stand-alone power unit, which came on-line in 1940. Perhaps the HEA was this motor designated specifically for the Model GTX.

A special-built crane, called a "crash crane," was designed to fit in tandem behind the Model GTX. Serial numbers for the crash crane indicated 20 units were manufactured.

As far as we know, no Model GTX vehicles exist in the United States, but it is rumored that one currently resides in Italy.

There was at least one prototype model made before production began, which looked more like the Model GT tractor than did the later units. The GTX was evaluated at the Aberdeen, Maryland, test facility in 1941. Differing from the MM company specifications, the Army called the GTX a 7 1/2-ton 6x6.

When this harvest scene near Climax, Michigan, was photographed in 1941, the equipment being used was state-of-the-art: Minneapolis-Moline Model UTU tractor and Model 69 Harvestor. Note the paint color, which isn't the orange shade of Prairie Gold used in later years. *Roger Mohr Collection*

The Avery V was continued in production by Minneapolis-Moline after purchase of the B. F. Avery & Sons Company in 1951. This tractor has an engine that develops 9 horsepower from 65 ci of displacement.

B. F. AVERY & SONS
JOINS THE LINE

On March 1, 1951, B. F. Avery & Sons Company of Louisville, Kentucky, merged with the MM firm, which became the surviving company. If timing is everything, the merger's timing tallied a "nothing" for all concerned.

Unfortunately, within 30 days the venture became a war casualty. It proved a sad fate for the products and facilities of B. F. Avery, a company whose history spanned 125 years, placing it among the country's oldest agricultural equipment manufacturers.

Founder Benjamin Franklin Avery was born in Aurora, New York, on December 3, 1801. In 1825 he moved to Clarksville, Virginia, where he started his first plow factory in a small log cabin. His partner, Calab H. Richmog, a practical molder, accompanied him in the move and in the new venture.

"An implement is not built until it is built right," was the motto established by the company, and a principle the company maintained throughout its long history.

From the beginning Avery's business prospered, but after some years the property owner refused to renew the lease and the firm moved to various locations but failed to find facilities that satisfied its needs.

Louisville, Kentucky, on the Ohio and Mississippi Rivers, offered excellent water transportation to the rural agricultural regions of the South. To take advantage of these benefits, the B. F. Avery & Sons Company relocated to a new factory at Preston and Main Streets in Louisville in December 1845.

Seven years later the company again

needed better and bigger facilities, so the firm moved to a larger plant at 15th and Main. This location was home for the firm until 1909, when the demand for its products once again necessitated larger production facilities. This time the company purchased 57 acres of land on South Seventh Street where a new plant was constructed. The plant was designed by George C. Avery, second son of B. F. Avery, who was connected with the business his entire life. He served 19 years as company president.

The size of the Louisville facility is somewhat uncertain as several archival sources are in conflict on this point. Its size is given as 38 or 57 acres of land with the plant covering 800,000, 830,000, or 900,000 square feet of floor space.

Avery products were sold throughout the world, and for many years the export markets played an important role in the company's growth. However, in 1932 the Argentine business, including a branch warehouse in Buenos Aires, was sold to the Allis-Chalmers Manufacturing Company.

The B. F. Avery firm signed a contract with Montgomery Ward & Company in 1939 giving that company distribution rights for Avery farm implements in territories not served by Avery branches and dealers. As of 1948, Avery maintained company branch houses in Dallas, Texas, and Memphis, Tennessee.

Also in 1939, Avery entered the power farming trend by building a line of tractor-drawn implements and contracting with an

Minneapolis-Moline started production of the BF in 1952, just a year after it bought out the Avery company. This 1956 BF has approximately 24 drawbar horsepower and provisions for a three-point hitch.

outside firm to build a tractor from Avery's design. The name of this outside firm is uncertain as is the design and type of tractor. Since Avery designed this tractor we would imagine it is similar to the Model A tractor that was later built in its own facility.

This interesting find: we don't know if it applies to this tractor found in C. H. Wendel's *Minneapolis-Moline Tractors 1870-1969:* "In a curious footnote, Junkin was working on the design for the B. F. Avery tractor at the time of his death in 1936." Jack Junkin was an engineer with MS&M and later with MM.

It is most likely that these first models of the Avery tractor were built by the Cleveland Tractor Company of Cleveland, Ohio. This company is best known for its line of crawlers, including the Cletrac. The only wheel tractor it produced was the General GG, and there seems to be little doubt that

this model is the tractor that was sold under the Avery name from 1939 through 1942.

In 1942, according to archival documents, the first Avery-built tractor, the Model A, was manufactured at the Avery facility. Serial number lists don't begin recording these tractors until 1943. We don't know why there is this discrepancy.

Along with the Model A came a complete line of Tru-Draft equipment for the tractor. The principle of Tru-Draft as applied to the Avery implements means they were hitched "from center-of-load to center-of-power." By attaching in this manner, the implements are allowed to float free of the tractor, and a minimum amount of power and fuel is required to pull the implements in their natural line of draft.

The Model V tractor along with a complete line of Tru-Draft equipment was

introduced in 1946. By 1948 the postwar boom required the manufacturing plant to run at full capacity anticipating the 1949 harvest. An archival document stated the daily output as 15 carloads of tractors and plows including cultivating and harvesting equipment.

MM's acquisition of Avery in 1951 gave MM five production units, with locations and size, under roof, as follows:

1. Hopkins Plant,
   Hopkins, Minnesota   820,000 sq. ft.
2. Lake St. Plant,
   Minneapolis, Minnesota 749,089 sq. ft.
3. Como Plant,
   Minneapolis, Minnesota 100,130 sq. ft.
4. Moline Plant,
   Moline, Illinois   1,019,000 sq. ft.
5. Avery Plant,
   Louisville, Kentucky   850,000 sq. ft.

It was a great concept that didn't quite catch on. The "Uni-Tractor" or "Uni-Farmor" was designed to mount and power various pieces of equipment such as picker-sheller, chopper, windrower, or baler. Using a 206-ci four-cylinder OHV engine, it developed 45 PTO horsepower. Attached to this Uni-Tractor is a Model 760 baler. This was a straight-through–type baler, from pickup to the bale's exit out the back, which is common in today's balers, but a novelty back then. This is one of the last versions of the Uni-Tractors which became known as the "Brown Mule" and was probably built in 1961 or 1962.

Prior to the merger, production during 1950 at the respective plants was:

Hopkins Plant

Harvestors	7,050
Shellers	1,500
Corn Pickers	5,150
Grain Drills	9,700
Windrowers	3,200

Lake Street Plant

Large farm and industrial tractors	20,404
Industrial unit engines	2,838

Como Plant

Automatic wire tie balers	2,522
Tractor-drawn mowers	5,000

Moline Plant

Tillage tools	86,000

With strong production from its own four facilities, MM expected to grow even faster utilizing the Avery plant. What it did not foresee was the Korean War, which led to government-imposed limitations on manufacturing materials and production. The restrictions would render MM's acquisition of Avery not only useless, but detrimental.

W.C. MacFarlane drafted a letter to shareholders to explain the unfortunate circumstances that followed the merger:

Recent publicity releases have announced the decision of the Management of your Company to dispose of the plant properties at Louisville. A brief explanation of the background of the properties would seem in order.

On March 1, 1951, Minneapolis-Moline acquired, by merger, the business and assets of B. F. Avery & Sons Company.

At the time of the merger, Minneapolis-Moline Company had just completed its fourth successive record-breaking year of sales and looked forward to an increasing volume of business in 1951 and 1952.

However, because of defense production requirements due to the Korean War, the Federal government, on March 31, 1951, instituted certain materials controls regulations affecting our production.

This 1947 Avery Model A was purchased by the present owner's grandfather in Urbana, Illinois, and has been in the family ever since. The IXB-3 Hercules four-cylinder engine delivers power through a three-speed transmission. This tractor has PTO, belt pulley, and hydraulic lift. The single front wheel was probably the most popular front axle configuration; however, a tricycle and adjustable wide front axle were available as an option. *Gregg Phillips*

Serial number 2V611 verifies that this Avery Model V was produced in 1948. The four-cylinder Hercules engine displaced 65 ci and was rated for 9 horsepower. This tractor has the optional PTO and belt pulley. An electric starter and lights were standard. *Russel Miner*

Cleveland Tractor Company of Cleveland, Ohio, built the General GG from 1939 through 1942. This 1939 model is typical of all General GGs. The four-cylinder Hercules engine is mated to a three-speed Clark transmission. Hand brakes were standard while options included a two-wheel tricycle front end and 6-volt electrical system with starter and lights. This same model was sold by Massey-Harris in Canada and by the Farmers Co-op in the States. The color scheme was known as Cletrac Orange. *Jim and Betty Parker*

These controls limited the amount of strategic raw materials such as steel, copper, rubber, etc., normally used in civilian production, including that of farm machinery, to a percentage based on a history of use during a base period prior to the Korean incident. Because of the low level of production at the Avery Plant prior to its acquisition, this production limitation proved drastic and immediately made it impossible to utilize the Louisville Plant for the expanded production anticipated at the time the merger was negotiated.

By the time the material controls were lifted late in 1953, the farm machinery market had deteriorated to the point where production schedules, instead of expanding as they might have in the spring of 1951, had to be drastically curtailed.

The farm market has not materially improved during the past two years. Therefore, to curtail losses that would be sustained in attempting to maintain that property until such time as increasing farm-machinery demands would expand its use, disposition of the plant seems in order at this time.

Continuing from the same letter he gives the grim reality of losses. "Operating the Louisville Plant resulted in a loss in 1952 of $606,000, a loss in 1953 of $2,113,000, a loss in 1954 of $407,000, a gain in 1955 to 8/31/55 of $88,000 before applying selling and administrative expenses."

An interesting note penciled on one of the archival documents stated that during the Civil War, 1861–1865, the B. F. Avery plant was used as a hospital by both armies. This facility, after a history of succoring the wounded and dying, was itself lost on account of war. Yet many of the tractors produced there live on.

Louisville Motor Plow: 1914–1917

Numerous documents giving the history of the B. F. Avery company reside in the Minnesota Historical Society archives. Many of these, we believe, were generated by the Avery company, yet not one of them mentions the Louisville Motor Plow, which it introduced in 1914. This would lead, for those who are prone to speculate, to the conclusion that it wasn't a resounding success. R. B. Gray wrote, "After a momentary success, sales fell off and its manufacture was discontinued in 1917."

Except for the red paint, this 1941 Wards Twin Row is the same tractor as the General GG. This tractor has a battery and starter that were offered to buyers as an option. *Russel Miner*

In design and concept it was similar to many pioneering tractors. It was a three-wheeler with the rear furrow wheel being the driver wheel. The two-cylinder opposed engine ran at 675 rpm and was rated as 10–20 horsepower. It featured one forward speed of 2 1/2 miles per hour.

Avery Model A: 1943–1950

Avery's line of tractors were small vehicles, aimed at the row-crop farming of the South, especially tobacco farms. The early Model A used a four-cylinder Hercules engine with a 3 1/8x4-inch bore and stroke. Later models switched to a Hercules IXB-3 with a 3 1/4x4-inch bore and stroke design. The Model A was a two-12-inch-blade plow tractor with a single front wheel and adjustable rear wheels.

Avery Model V: 1946–1952

The Model V was a one-plow model with a ZXB-3 Hercules engine and a 3/1

transmission. The ZXB-3 four-cylinder engine was designed with 2 5/8x3-inch bore and stroke.

This was a standard tread tractor with a channel iron frame with a front cross-member for attaching the Tru-Draft implements.

Avery R: 1950–1952

The Model R was introduced in 1950 and, instead of the previous three-speed transmission, used a four-speed design. Sometime in 1952, the paint scheme was changed from Avery red to Prairie Gold. Also in 1952 the model designation became the BF.

MM BF: 1952–1953

This model was available in three different front axle configurations: BFS as a single front wheel, BFD as a dual wheel tricycle, and BFW as a wide adjustable front axle. Adjustment on the BFW front axle was from 52 inches to 72 inches. All models had adjustable rear tread from 52 inches to 76 inches in 4-inch steps.

Special rear tires and modified front axle transformed the BF into the BFH Hi-Crop model with 27 1/2-inch crop clearance. Both front and rear tread was adjustable to the same widths as the other BF models.

All models used a four-cylinder IXB3SL 133-ci Hercules engine with a 3 1/4x4-inch bore and stroke with variable governing from 1,200 to 1,800 rpm. Horsepower fell in the 25 range at the drawbar. A 4/1 transmission allowed forward travel of 1.6 to 13 miles per hour.

In 1953 the serial numbers changed from the Avery system to the MM system and after the merger until 1952 the tractors shared the MM Avery badge. With the model BG, the Avery name disappeared from the BG and BF tractors.

MM BG: 1953–1955

Also using the Hercules engine, this time the 1X3SL with 133-ci displacement, it generated 25 horsepower and used a 4/1 trans-

This crawler bears Avery decals and sheet metal, but there is some question whether or not Avery actually built a crawler. This crawler has the same Hercules engine, Clark transmission and frame as the BF Avery Model A. The owner considers this a 1948 Avery Model A crawler. He believes Avery purchased the vehicle, less tin work, form Cleveland Tractor Company and fitted it with Avery tin and colors. *Jim and Betty Parker*

mission. The BG was a one-row outfit and the off-set steering design gave excellent visibility of the crop being worked.

MM Uni-Tractor: 1951–1963

Introduced in 1951, the Uni-Tractor is a self-propelled carrier and power source for a number of harvesting implements. Collectively, this exclusive MM system is called the Uni-Farmor. Attachments include the Uni-Foragor for harvesting hay and forage crops, a Uni-Windrower that cuts and windrows hay and grain, Uni-Harvestor, which combines grain crops, and the Uni-Huskor to

pick corn. Picking and shelling in one operation is handled by the Uni-Picker-Sheller.

The Uni-Huskor won first, second, third, and sixth places at the 1954 International Corn Picking Contest.

From its introduction in 1951 through 1954, the Uni-Tractors used the V206-4 engine. In 1955 through part of 1960 it was produced with the V206B-4 upgrade engine, and sometime in 1960 through 1963 it switched to the 206N-4 model engine. During 1961 and 1962 it was offered with a D206B-4 diesel engine. PTO horsepower fell in the 45 range.

This unique power carrier and its implements were manufactured at the Como facility from 1951 through 1954, at which time production was moved to the Hopkins plant and stayed there from 1955 to 1963.

After 13 years of production under the MM badge, the Uni-Farmor design was sold to the New Idea Company in 1963.

During 1962 and 1963, the Government Chemical Corps purchased just over 50 of these units. We don't know exactly why, but it has been suggested that they used them for chemical application on military bases.

The restorer calls this 1959 model his "Baby Rattler" because it rattles so much when driven. This 445 Utility Diesel was powered by a diesel engine that was factory observed at 50 brake horsepower. It, too, offered as an option the 10/2 Ampli-Torc that in essence doubled the number of transmission speeds and provided more lugging power in tough spots.

LAST OF THE PRAIRIE GOLD TRACTORS

The debut of the MM Model 335 and Model 445 also marked the introduction of the company's Powerlined Series of tractors. From this point on, with the exception of the GVI and G700 Series, every MM-built tractor had a 5/1 transmission with the 10/2 Ampli-Torc as either standard equipment or available as an option.

MM 335 Utility: 1956–1961

The Model 335 was introduced as a "gasoline only" model but shortly thereafter an LP gas version was in production. The same 165A-4 engine was used in both tractors. The 165-ci MM-made engine operated at 1,600 rpm and Nebraska test number 624 certified that the 335 gasoline model produced 29 drawbar and 33 belt horsepower.

Specification sheets list two different groups of features customers could choose from to customize a Model 335 for their needs. The extra equipment included PTO, auxiliary PTO located under the transmission for side- and front-mounted equipment, belt pulley, rear wheel weights, front wheel weights, and a built-in hydraulic unit with cylinder.

The Model 335 Utility front axle was adjustable from 48 inches to 76 inches. A heavy I-beam front axle nearly identical to that used on the RTI was optional. Power adjustable rear wheels were also offered in the option category. Additional options included a bevy of hydraulic equipment: remote jack, breakaway hose couplings, power steering, three-point hitch, and exterior

PTO-driven hydraulic pumps, as well as a special axle for light loader work.

Also under options was the 10/2 Ampli-Torc transmission drive, which the company literature describes this way, "By eliminating frequent clutching, stopping, shifting, and starting, Ampli-Torc helps you do 20 percent more work. Use high range for average field work; and when the going gets heavy, double your power by dropping into low range. Ampli-Torc provides 10 forward and two reverse speeds."

In 1957 the Universal, or tricycle, model of the 335 tractor was introduced and stayed in the line through 1959. Other than the front axle and rear wheel size this tractor shared the same specifications as the Utility model.

The Model 335 Industrial Wheel Tractor was produced from 1957 through 1960 and was basically the same as the agricultural Utility model with a few exceptions. Initially the standard transmission offered was the five-speed.

Early in production the shuttle transmission, which allowed five forward and five reverse speeds with the reverse being a bit faster than the forward travel speeds, became available. It appears that the shuttle tranny became standard equipment on late-production units. Other standard equipment on the Industrial version was a foot accelerator and hand throttle.

MM 445 Utility: 1956–1959

A little-bit-bigger brother would describe the Model 445 as compared to the Model 335—

A quite rare combination is this 1957 335 with side-mounted mower. It featured a four-cylinder inline OHV engine. Live power PTO, power steering, and the 10/2 Ampli-Torc transmission were available as an option.

The 335 and 445, such as this 445 model, introduced the 10/2 Ampli-Torc transmission providing 10 forward speeds. It was an option to the 5/1 transmission that was an MM hallmark for so many years.

Rakish-looking, this 1958 5 Star superseded the UB Special. It mounts a 283-ci engine that rated 49 drawbar and 54 belt horsepower in Nebraska tests. Although it was originally introduced as the 550 to follow the 335 and 445, its designation was changed to 5 Star. Its restorer, who's used one in the field, notes that "It's a really good workhorse of a tractor."

approximately seven more horses to do the work. Styling and most features were the same on both tractors, except the Model 445 made a 12-volt electrical system standard equipment.

Introduced at the same time was the Model 445 Universal. Tested at Nebraska, test number 578, it demonstrated drawbar horsepower of 38 and belt of 41 operating on gasoline. The Powerlined Series was available across the board in LP gas and you could specify tractor fuel if that was your fuel of choice.

An option on the Universal model was the Quick-Change front-end assembly, which allowed changing to the single front

wheel or to the wide adjustable front axle.

It is interesting to note that the 445 Universal is actually a longer tractor than the Utility and Industrial models. An extra 4 or 5 inches are built into the clutch housing area.

In 1958 only, the Model 445 Universal Diesel joined the line with the D206-4 four-cylinder engine. MM estimated the net brake horsepower at 50. The Model 445 diesels used two 12-volt batteries for faster cold weather starts.

The Model 445 Utility Diesel is a rare tractor as only 18 copies were produced in 1959, the only year it was manufactured. It

shared the same specs and styling as the Universal model diesel.

The gasoline and LP gas Industrial version was manufactured from 1956 through 1958 and the diesel model Industrial in 1958 only. Both were available with the standard 5/1, the Ampli-Torc, or the shuttle transmission.

Also manufactured as the Model 445 Military vehicle, it was fitted with a larger M220A-4 engine. Only 74 of these tractors were produced.

MM 5 Star: 1957–1960
Originally designated the Model 550, this

The 4 Star Super tractor included as standard equipment Ampli-Torc, Tel-O-Flo hydraulics, and power steering. This 1960 model developed 39 drawbar and 44 PTO horsepower according to Nebraska tests. The consensus is that it just has to be one of the sleekest tractors ever designed.

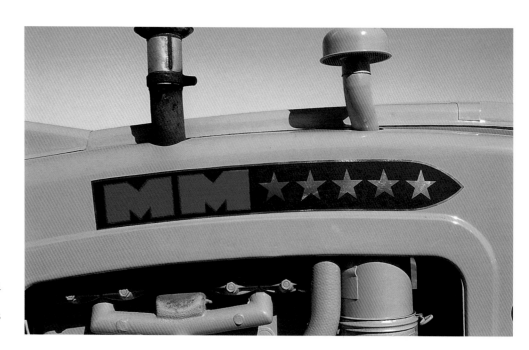

Although some people might consider this a little too much for a macho tractor, the 5 Star model designation certainly won points for its distinctive and eye-catching decal.

The M-5's 336 engine with 4 5/8x5-inch bore and stroke enabled M-5s, such as this 1961 model, to supply 54 horsepower at the drawbar and 61 at the PTO according to Nebraska test results.

tractor was renamed when another manufacturer pointed out that it already had a 550 model in its line. So MM chose the name "5 Star" instead. The 5 Star replaced the UB models in the MM wheeled tractor lineup. Its styling closely followed the look of the Model 335 and Model 445 tractors.

The Universal gasoline and LP gas models were introduced in 1957 and were made through 1959. Both used the 283E-4 engine, and the LP gas model was tested at Nebraska, test number 651 in 1958, and rated 49 and 54 horsepower, respectively, at the drawbar and belt. The 5 Star Universal Diesel, made during the same years, used MM's D336-4 engine. In Nebraska test number 652 in 1958, it achieved the same power ratings as the LP model.

All the Universal Models could be converted to type "N" or type "E" front axles.

Type "E," or extendable, front axles were adjustable from 52 to 76 inches.

The gasoline and LP gas Standard Models were produced only in 1958 and the diesel engine model was available in both 1958 and 1959. Standard models had a fixed front wheel tread of 51 3/8 inches.

MM still continued to offer, as an option, engines equipped to burn tractor fuel if that was the customer's preference.

Common to all the 5 Star models is a 12-volt electrical system, keyed ignition, pressurized cooling system, oil bath air cleaner, sealed beam headlights, cigarette lighter, speedometer, and a cushion seat with backrest.

Ampli-Torc 10-speed transmission, independent PTO, built-in power steering, and power adjust rear wheels were also

available. Any standard three-point implements could be mounted on the hydraulic three-point hitch. The Tel-O-Flo hydraulic system could accommodate two remote-control cylinders in addition to the three-point system.

There were 84 copies of the 5 Star Industrial gasoline tractor produced from 1957 through 1959. The diesel version of the 5 Star Industrial was made in 1958, 1959, and 1960, totaling only 60 units.

MM Jet Star: 1959–1962

The Jet Star models were introduced while the Model 335 was still in production even though it was seen as a replacement for the Model 335. A noted collector said that the Jet Star was a "bare bones tractor—an engine and four wheels."

Here's the designer's concept in the early l960s for the Jet Star Series tractors. As far as is known, no prototypes were ever made of this design. The Motec logo probably dates this model sometime between 1961 and 1963. *Roger Mohr Collection*

The first Jet Stars marked a departure from the standard Prairie Gold color scheme. These vehicles were entirely metallic bronze with Prairie Gold wheels. The Jet Star 2 and Jet Star 3 tractors featured a lighter yellow tin work, known as Energy Yellow, with Dyna Brown chassis.

MM's factory tests put the horsepower rating of the Jet Star at 44 drawbar and 48 PTO with the gasoline engine. The engine was the 206-ci Type 206L-4 with a 3 5/8x5-inch bore and stroke. The same engine was used for the LP gas version. The Ampli-Torc 10/2

transmission was an option in place of the standard 5/1. A reversible front axle provided for a shorter wheelbase and turning radius.

Only for the year 1961 did MM offer an Orchard Model of the Jet Star. Collectors might come across serial numbers that would indicate earlier Orchard tractors. "Boozer" conversions are the explanation for this seeming contradiction. Boozer's Service and Equipment, Inc. of Winter Haven, Florida, began converting the Jet Star to an Orchard tractor, probably in 1960, to provide Orchard models for the area's citrus grove farmers.

Later this became a joint effort between Boozer and MM. These conversion tractors will carry the Jet Star serial number prefix 165 and were manufactured during regular Jet Star production. Fifty MM factory production Orchard models appeared in 1961 with their own serial number, prefix 220. These production models were tagged "Jet Star, Orchard Type, Gasoline or LP, Package #57." Undoubtedly some of these were sent to Florida as part of the joint effort with Boozer Implement and some also went to Michigan and New York for use by apple growers.

This 1955 prototype of a 445 utility tractor was never manufactured in this design. There were also 445 prototype row-crop gasoline and diesel versions developed. *Roger Mohr Collection*

Company literature lists the following as standard equipment for the Orchard Jet Star: Independent PTO, swinging drawbar, front radiator grille guard, engine side enclosures, complete rear fender cowling, heavy front axle, low operator's position, 10-speed Ampli-Torc transmission, no hydraulics, and LP gas or gasoline MM-built engines.

It isn't known just how many early Boozer conversions were made. They did have the same paint scheme as the factory tractors—metallic bronze with Prairie Gold wheels.

In the 1980s the above-mentioned collector was in Florida and decided to look for some MM Orchard tractors. He located a citrus grove owner who had used the same fleet of MM Orchard tractors for 20 years. The owner then decided to replace the fleet with a foreign-built tractor. These new tractors lasted just one year. So, they bought a new fleet of a major U.S.-brand orchard tractors. These lasted two years. Unfortunately the rugged MM Jet Stars were no longer being produced. However, it's quite a testament to the durability of this MM product.

The Jet Star Diesel appeared in 1960 with a D206-4 engine. Other specs mimicked the gasoline and LP gas models. The last year of production for the diesel was 1962.

MM 4 Star: 1959–1963

The 4 Star was similar to the Jet Star but with a few more "goodies." Both used the same 206L-4 engine for gasoline or LP gas, but the 4 Star had the Ampli-Torc transmission as standard equipment. There was also a color difference, with the 4 Star carrying the darker Prairie Gold tin work and wheels matched to a metallic bronze chassis.

Three-point hitch, Tel-O-Flo hydraulic system, and power steering are some of the

The 550 designation on this sleek tractor was changed after only a few were produced because that model number was already being used by another manufacturer. So the model designation was changed to 5 Star shortly after the first models were released. *Roger Mohr Collection*

goodies that were standard equipment on the 4 Star. It could be ordered with the single wheel, the dual wheel tricycle, or the wide adjustable front axle.

The 4 Star Diesel came on-line in 1960 and was produced through 1962 using the D206-4 MM-built engine.

The 4 Star Super was available concurrently with the 4 Star and shared the same serial number prefix for both the diesel and gasoline/LP gas models so we can't determine the number made of each model.

The Supers were just a deluxe version of the 4 Star with extra standard equipment such as power adjusted rear wheels, crown fenders, dual headlights, new drawbar, and transistorized alternator.

MM GVI: 1959–1962

Previously the "big" tractor slot in the MM line was covered by the Model GB. With the

introduction of the Model GVI, the GB bowed out to a bigger and better-equipped tractor.

Three fuel options were available with the six-cylinder 425-ci engine: gasoline, LP gas, and diesel. Probably about 99 percent of the nondiesel production was LP gas.

The gasoline and LP gas tractors had the 425B-6 engine while the diesel carried the

D425A-6; bore and stroke on both engine types was 4 1/4x5-inch while the governed rpm was 1,500.

The LP gas model and the diesel model were Nebraska-tested in 1961. Test number 791 placed the LP gas horsepower as 71 at the drawbar and 78 at the PTO, while test number 792 showed the diesel version to generate 68 drawbar and 78 PTO horsepower.

The transmission was 5/1 with a hand clutch. The Model GVI was a fixed front axle. Standard equipment included power steering and a 12-volt electrical system. The gasoline and LP gas models used two 12-volt batteries and the diesel used three. The system included two sealed beam headlights, two combination floodlights, taillights, and an auxiliary connector socket.

LP gas and diesel versions were produced for Massey-Ferguson, where they became the Model MF-95 Super. The MF tractors carried their own serial number, which can be found in the Appendix serial number list.

There was a dealer package available to convert the Model GVI to a front-wheel-assist four-wheel-drive unit.

The Model GVI offered improved operator comfort including a high platform, full crown fenders, and front platform plates to keep the operator somewhat out of the dust. Company advertising advised that "You have to get into the seat of a Moline tractor to fully appreciate what Moline Control Zone Comfort means." Besides the new high platform,

This prototype 5 Star model, which started design life as a 550, utilized a German-made Bosch injector pump. However, American-made Bosch injector pumps were installed on all regular production tractors. *Roger Mohr Collection*

Live power in all four wheels was said to boost pulling power of the G-704 tractor by up to 50 percent and enable it to pull up to nine plow bottoms. *Roger Mohr Collection*

the company touted Finger-Touch Steering, Flote-Ride Seat, "Natural Direction" hand clutch, and High Leverage brakes.

MM M5: 1960–1963

This model looks a lot like the Model GVI, with the same styling, same colors, and same Moline Control Zone Comfort operator's platform. But the M5 is smaller in engine size, wheelbase, and horsepower.

Nebraska tests, numbers 756 and 757, placed both the gasoline and LP gas tractors at 54 drawbar and 61 PTO horsepower. Both vehicles used the 336-4 engine with 4 5/8x5-inch bore and stroke.

The D336-4 diesel engine with the same bore and stroke powered the Model M5 Diesel when it was tested at Nebraska, with results of 51 drawbar and 58 PTO horsepower.

The Ampli-Torc transmission was standard on all models of the M5, giving 10 forward speeds from 1.7 to 18 miles per hour.

Probably most production was in the Universal, or tricycle, models; however, the three interchangeable front-end styles—single wheel, dual wheel, or wide extendable—were available as an option. Otherwise the standard, and option, package was similar to the Model GVI. As with the Model GVI, dealer conversions to front-wheel assist were available.

MM M504: 1962 only

This was a factory-built, four-wheel-drive version of the Model M5, which was nearly identical to the dealer-converted four-wheel tractors. M504s had their own serial numbers whereas the conversions, of course, did not. This definitely wasn't a high-volume production tractor: only 10 copies of the gasoline or LP gas version and 21 copies of the diesel model made it off the assembly line.

MM G704: 1962 only

This was a full-time four-wheel-drive version of the Model GVI. It was also sold under the Massey-Ferguson banner as the four-wheel-drive Model MF-95 Super.

MINNEAPOLIS MOLINE* G-704 4-Wheel Drive TRACTOR

Increases pulling power up to 50%

LIVE POWER in ALL 4 WHEELS!

- Increases drawbar pull 30 to 50%
- Pulls up to 9 plows
- More pulling power per gallon of fuel
- Pulls up steep slopes, through mud
- Needs less wheel weights
- Causes less soil compaction
- Uses full power on turns
- Longer tire wear due to less slippage
- Less wear on gears, shafts, bearings

MINNEAPOLIS-MOLINE • Hopkins, Minnesota
Moline Dealers give the best service in the industry

Minneapolis-Moline took a back seat to the Mocraft name in identifying this garden tractor of the 1960s to potential buyers. This lawn tractor featured a 36-inch mower deck and a 7-horsepower Kohler engine.

MOTEC INDUSTRIES, INC

Motec was originally created as a subsidiary of MM. Yet the top brass were interested in pursuing a broader market than just agriculture. As a result they soon flipped the names, making Motec Industries, Inc., the parent company over several divisions, including Minneapolis-Moline Farm Machinery. Motec was located in Hopkins, Minnesota.

The 1961 *Annual Report* explains that "The change of name to Motec Industries, Inc. from Minneapolis-Moline Company and the creation of a new trademark signified the acceleration of a diversification program."

The name Motec is derived from "Moline technology." In 1961 the divisions of Motec Industries, Inc. included Minneapolis-Moline Farm Machinery, Mopower Construction Equipment, Mobilift Materials Handling, Mohawk Foundry & Forge, Motec International, Motec Electronics, Moline Automotive, Motec Engineering, and Mocraft.

The Farm Machinery division included Minneapolis-Moline and Mocraft. As described in the 1961 *Annual Report*, MM "produce[d] and distribute[d] a complete line of agricultural tractors, implements and harvesting equipment and in addition, the Uni-Farmor line of self-propelled machines." Mocraft was a new division specializing in "a variety of implements and tools for farm, suburban and estate use."

The Industrial division had six components, Mobilift, Mohawk, Moline Automotive, Mopower, Motec Electronics, and Motec Engineering, which the company report described as follows.

"MOBILIFT produces a family of cushion-tired and pneumatic-tired fork lift trucks and towing tractors of various capacities for gasoline and LP gas, as well as a special series of highly maneuverable stand-up fork lift trucks.

"MOHAWK provides contract manufacturing of castings, forgings, machining, metal fabrication and other specialized precision work for industry and government.

"MOLINE AUTOMOTIVE products include a broad range of gasoline, LP gas, diesel and natural gas engines for oil field and irrigation use; and "power trains" which consist of engine, transmission, hydraulic steering system and axle for original equipment manufacturers and a wide variety of industrial applications. Moline Automotive also provides custom engineering and consulting services.

"MOPOWER builds a line of industrial tractors and attachments for construction industry, road building, housing and utility operations.

"MOTEC ELECTRONICS (located in Los Angeles, California) designs and manufactures electronic air safety test equipment for the aircraft industry, as well as other electronic components.

"MOTEC ENGINEERING provides custom engineering service in design and manufacture of precision tools, dies, jigs and fixtures for industry and for other divisions of Motec Industries."

The third division was Motec International, which distributed the company's

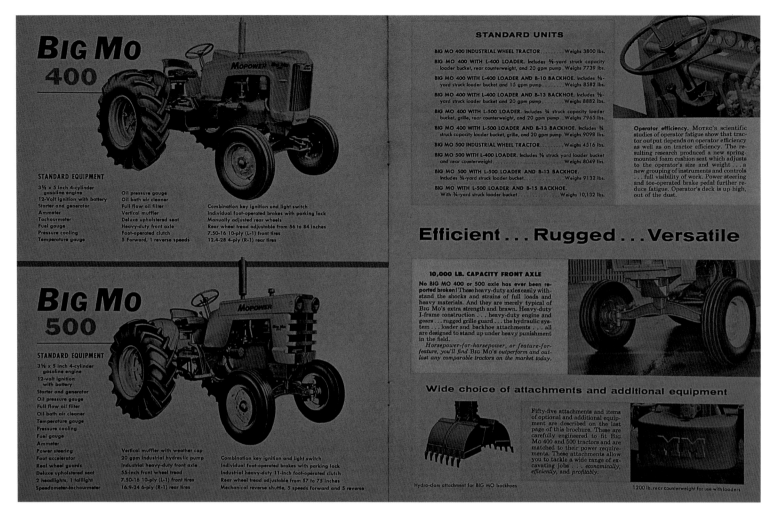

BIG MO 400

STANDARD EQUIPMENT

3½ x 5 inch 4-cylinder
  gasoline engine
12-Volt ignition with battery
Starter and generator
Ammeter
Tachourmeter
Fuel gauge
Pressure cooling
Temperature gauge

Oil pressure gauge
Oil bath air cleaner
Full flow oil filler
Vertical muffler
Deluxe upholstered seat
Heavy-duty front axle
Foot-operated clutch
5 Forward, 1 reverse speeds

Combination key ignition and light switch
Individual foot-operated brakes with parking lock
Manually adjusted rear wheels
Rear wheel tread adjustable from 56 to 84 inches
7.50-16 10-ply (L-1) front tires
12.4-28 4-ply (R-1) rear tires

BIG MO 500

STANDARD EQUIPMENT

3½ x 5 inch 4-cylinder
  gasoline engine
12-volt ignition
  with battery
Starter and generator
Oil pressure gauge
Full flow oil filler
Oil bath air cleaner
Temperature gauge
Pressure cooling
Fuel gauge
Ammeter
Power steering
Foot accelerator
Real wheel guards
Deluxe upholstered seat
2 headlights, 1 taillight
Speedometer-tachourmeter

Vertical muffler with weather cap
20 gpm industrial hydraulic pump
Industrial heavy-duty front axle
55-inch front wheel tread
7.50-16 10-ply (L-1) front tires
16.9-24 6-ply (R-1) rear tires

Combination key ignition and light switch
Individual foot-operated brakes with parking lock
Industrial heavy-duty 11-inch foot-operated clutch
Rear wheel tread adjustable from 57 to 75 inches
Mechanical reverse shuttle, 5 speeds forward and 5 reverse

STANDARD UNITS

BIG MO 400 INDUSTRIAL WHEEL TRACTOR........ Weighs 3800 lbs.

BIG MO 400 WITH L-400 LOADER. Includes ½-yard struck capacity
  loader bucket, rear counterweight, and 20 gpm pump. Weighs 7739 lbs.

BIG MO 400 WITH L-400 LOADER AND B-10 BACKHOE. Includes ½-
  yard struck loader bucket and 15 gpm pump........ Weighs 8582 lbs.

BIG MO 400 WITH L-400 LOADER AND B-13 BACKHOE. Includes ½-
  yard struck loader bucket and 20 gpm pump........ Weighs 8882 lbs.

BIG MO 400 WITH L-500 LOADER. Includes ¾ struck capacity loader
  bucket, grille, rear counterweight, and 20 gpm pump. Weighs 7965 lbs.

BIG MO 400 WITH L-500 LOADER AND B-13 BACKHOE. Includes ¾
  struck capacity loader bucket, grille, and 20 gpm pump. Weighs 9098 lbs.

BIG MO 500 INDUSTRIAL WHEEL TRACTOR........ Weighs 4516 lbs.

BIG MO 500 WITH L-400 LOADER. Includes ½ struck yard loader bucket
  and rear counterweight...................... Weighs 8049 lbs.

BIG MO 500 WITH L-500 LOADER AND B-13 BACKHOE.
  Includes ¾-yard struck loader bucket........ Weighs 9132 lbs.

BIG MO WITH L-500 LOADER AND B-15 BACKHOE.
  With ¾-yard struck loader bucket............ Weighs 10,132 lbs.

Operator efficiency. Motec's scientific studies of operator fatigue show that tractor output depends on operator efficiency as well as on tractor efficiency. The resulting research produced a new spring-mounted foam cushion seat which adjusts to the operator's size and weight . . . a new grouping of instruments and controls . . . full visibility of work. Power steering and toe-operated brake pedal further reduce fatigue. Operator's deck is up high, out of the dust.

Efficient . . . Rugged . . . Versatile

10,000 LB. CAPACITY FRONT AXLE
No BIG MO 400 or 500 axle has ever been reported broken! These heavy-duty axles easily withstand the shocks and strains of full loads and heavy materials. And they are merely typical of Big Mo's extra strength and brawn. Heavy-duty I-frame construction . . . heavy-duty engine and gears . . . rugged grille guard . . . the hydraulic system . . . loader and backhoe attachments . . . all are designed to stand up under heavy punishment in the field.
  Horsepower-for-horsepower, or feature-for-feature, you'll find Big Mo's outperform and outlast any comparable tractors on the market today.

Wide choice of attachments and additional equipment

Fifty-five attachments and items of optional and additional equipment are described on the last page of this brochure. These are carefully engineered to fit Big Mo 400 and 500 tractors and are matched to their power requirements. These attachments allow you to tackle a wide range of excavating jobs . . . *economically, efficiently, and profitably.*

Hydro-clam attachment for BIG MO backhoes

1200 lb. rear counterweight for use with loaders

BIG MO 400 and 500 models were industrial tractors aimed at various facets of the construction business. In general, due to the harshness of the conditions in which they worked, these tractors were more heavily built than the tractors designed for farm use. *Dennis Parker Collection*

products outside the United States and Canada "marketed through franchised distributors, affiliates and subsidiaries."

The company name change and the shuffling of divisions had brief significance. Motec lasted only until January 1, 1963, when it was purchased by White Motor Company.

The BIG MO Models were introduced in the Motec years. All BIG MO units were industrial tractors. The company also produced lawn and garden tractors during this period, within the Mocraft division. From sometime in 1961 through an undetermined date in 1963, many, but not all, MM tractors carried Motec I.D. plates.

BIG MO 500: 1960–1966

Here we have the Industrial version of the 4 Star farm tractor. The 206-ci engine

is the same, the tin work is the same, but the standard fixed front axle is heavier than the agricultural model. These Industrial models had a silver gray chassis instead of the metallic bronze of the agricultural tractors.

The standard equipment transmission is a 5/5 mechanical shuttle with a top speed forward and reverse of 14.57 and 18.22, respectively. The Ampli-Torc 10/2 was offered as a factory-installed option.

For the first year of production, these wheelers had the same grille as the agricultural tractor but in later models they got their own heavy cast-iron grille. On the gasoline model, this change occurred at serial number 16800161, while the diesel model was changed at serial number 17800066.

The diesel model was offered from 1960 through 1965.

BIG MO 600: 1960 only

A few changes were effected to transform the BIG MO 500 into the BIG MO 600. The same engine was upped from 1,750 to 2,000 rpm and the 5/5 shuttle transmission was hydraulic as opposed to mechanical. Actually it was the same tranny as was used in the 2 Star and Motrac crawlers. It was produced with a gasoline engine and only 60 copies came off the assembly line.

BIG MO 400: 1961–1964

This was an Industrial model of the Jet Star farm tractor fitted with a 5/5 shuttle transmission. It carried the 206L-4 engine.

Axles and wheels were beefed up for the continual loader and blade work encountered on industrial application. This, too, was a gasoline-only model.

BIG MO
400 TRACTOR

BIG MO 500 WITH
L-500 LOADER

BIG MO 500 WITH
B-15 BACKHOE

BIG MO

400 AND 500 SERIES
TRACTORS, LOADERS
and BACKHOES

MOTEC

Bulletin 1071

TRACTORS
LOADERS
BACKHOES

CONVENIENT PAYMENTS TO SUIT YOUR
NEEDS THROUGH

GENERAL ELECTRIC
CREDIT CORPORATION

This BIG MO brochure cover instantly informed the construction buyer that he could do some one-stop shopping when he bought either the 400 or 500 model. There was no need to look elsewhere for an accompanying loader or backhoe. *Dennis Parker Collection*

This 1961 garden tractor carrying the 110 designation and straddling a lawn mower deck is still being used every summer by a restorer of MM tractors. His thought: Why bring in something else, when this one fits in so well and has years of useful service left?

BIG MO 400 Military: 1959–1963

To make the BIG MO 400 into a Military vehicle, the engine was changed to the M220A-4 as opposed to the smaller 206L-4. It had the standard 5/1 transmission, but no shuttle.

The were other minor alterations. The gas tank was changed from the styled standard design to a "big round can." A stamped metal pan seat replaced the cushion seat, and in case of an emergency it could be started with a crank that fit where the rear PTO was located on the agricultural tractor.

Lawn and Garden Tractors

Keeping in step with management's commitment to diversify, Motec introduced its line of lawn mowers, complete with an impressive line of attachments and implements, in 1962. Lawn mowers fell within the

96

newly created division of Mocraft, which was responsible for products aimed at farm, suburban, and estate use.

Even during the years when agricultural equipment sales were on the negative side of the ledger, lawn mowers continued to be offered and then made the transition to the White brand name in 1971. After 1963, all models shared very similar styling.

MM didn't manufacture lawn mowers but rather outsourced them from Jacobsen Manufacturing Company of Racine, Wisconsin. Most, if not all, attachments and implements were also outsourced from other vendors.

MM Mocraft: 1962–1963

Powered by a 7-horsepower Kohler engine, this unit came with an electric starter and a 36-inch mower deck. The paint scheme was either dark brown with white on the

hood sides, or entirely dark brown similar to the Dyna Brown of the agricultural tractors.

What's really impressive is the option and equipment package for these small tractors. Available were the following: 42-inch dozer blade, 10-inch plow, eight-disc disc, snow blower/auger, straddle cultivator, dump trailer, wheel weights, chains, lawn roller, lawn aerator, five-section reel mower, angle broom, headlights, hubcaps, and dual rear wheels.

A PTO was also available for powering a grain elevator, an auger, or even a generator to run a dairy's milking machines. A nice twist on these options could be the tax break provided to farm equipment purchases.

MM 107 Town and Country: 1963–1968

The Model 107 used a 7-horsepower

Minneapolis-Moline Crawlers

Crawler production was not a priority at MM, but the company did explore the design of a crawler to go along with the Industrial tractors. Prototypes were first fabricated in 1956, and by 1961 the crawler era closed at the MM company. Total production numbered just 250 vehicles plus one documented experimental crawler.

Evolution of the 2 Star crawler began in 1956 by marrying a D-2 Cat undercarriage to a Model 445 agricultural frame, engine, and powertrain. The tin work, seat, and operator's platform were vintage Model 445. The serial number allotted for this unit was X253.

The next experimental prototype was developed over MM's own fabricated undercarriage. Other changes were also made, such as a heavy industrial grille guard, appropriate tin work, and a wide bench seat that incorporated the fuel tank.

Although not known for producing crawler tractors, MM did produce the Motrac crawler, of which this 1957 model is a good example.

Production of the 2 Star Crawler began and ended in 1958. It was available in gasoline only and had a 206K-4 engine.

The redesigned Motrac Crawler came along in 1960 and 1961 in both gasoline and diesel engines. The gasoline version used the 206M-4 engine while the diesel type was a D206A-4.

This attractive-looking crawler tractor was another design concept that never saw daylight in prototype form. *Roger Mohr Collection*

Tecumseh engine, making it the only MM lawn tractor not powered by a Kohler power plant. It was available with a recoil as well as the electric starter and was fitted with a 34-inch mower deck.

All the same options and equipment listed for the Mocraft were available for the Model 107.

MM 108 Town and Country: 1964–1971

Power on this model was upped to 8 horsepower from a Kohler engine with an electric starter. However, the mower deck remained at 36 inches. The paint scheme was yellow with white hood sides, white wheels, and a white seat.

In addition to the Mocraft options and equipment, several more goodies were available including a hydraulic lift, hydraulic front loader, 30-inch front reel mower, spiked aerator, 32-inch tiller with its own engine, 48-inch side-mount sickle mower, and a canvas cab enclosure.

MM 110 Town and Country: 1964–1971

Sporting two more horses thanks to a 10-horsepower Kohler, this model came with a 36-inch deck until 1966, when a 42-inch and 48-inch deck became available. All of the equipment and options for the Model 108 model could be purchased for the 110 model.

Beginning with the 1966 models, a hydrostatic drive was fitted to the Model 110 giving it infinite variable speed forward and reverse travel. This was a top-of-the-line lawn and garden tractor equipped with headlights and taillights as a standard feature. And, if the customers wanted a cigarette lighter, horn, and hubcaps, all they had to do was ask for them.

MM 112 Town and Country: 1966–1971

Another deluxe package, powered by a 12-horsepower Kohler engine, the Model 112 was available with either a standard transmission or hydrostatic drive. In addition to the normal equipment, this tractor could be ordered with three different size tire options.

MM 114 Town and Country: 1969–1971

The 14-horsepower Model 114 was only available with hydrostatic drive. In addition to a hydraulic lift, it could be fitted with an electric lift for raising and lowering mounted or attached equipment.

A "user-friendly" feature of the MM line of lawn mowers allowed any deck from any model to be interchanged.

The Model 114 made the transition to the White banner as the White Model 114 outfitted in blue and white colors.

This 1965 U302 managed to extract quite a bit of power from an engine displacing only 220 ci. Drawbar horsepower was 49 and PTO horsepower was 55 when tested at Nebraska. Owner-installed modifications add a nice touch to this restored tractor.

LAST OF THE TRUE MINNEAPOLIS-MOLINE TRACTORS

White Motor Corporation purchased Motec Industries, Inc. on January 1, 1963, for $42 million. At this time MM was structured as a subsidiary of Motec.

Almost immediately after the acquisition there began to be a noticeable White influence on the tractors. White had purchased the Oliver concern in 1960 and the Cockshutt Company in 1962. These acquisitions also influenced White's treatment of the MM tractors.

MM U302: 1964–1965

Brought on-line to replace the 4 Star tractors, the Model U302 used the 220A-4 engine with 14 more ci displacement than the 4 Star engine. Bore and stroke on the 220A-4 was 3 3/4x5 inches with 1,900 governed rpm.

At Nebraska, test number 862, this combination certified 49 drawbar and 55 PTO horsepower using gasoline as the fuel. LP gas, test number 863, registered the same horsepower results—49 and 55.

This horsepower was channeled through the Ampli-Torc transmission providing the operator with a choice of 10 forward speeds ranging from 1.72 to 18.46 miles per hour and two reverse speeds at 2.73 and 5.05 miles per hour.

The tin work styling was the same as the Model M602 and painted Energy Yellow, including wheels, while the chassis was Dyna Brown. Carrying the rating of a three/four plow row-crop tractor it was available with either of three front axles—"U" dual tricycle,

"E" wide adjustable, or "N" single front wheel—plus the standard front axle.

In 1966 the Model U302 was upgraded to the Super model giving the MM lineup a row-crop tractor with full four-plow power. You can spot a Super, if it's restored correctly, by the new style grille without the narrow white band, but instead a broad white band around the hood.

Someone at MM did a little number crunching to show how the relatively low-rpm MM engines compared with the competition. These findings revealed that every 100 million revolutions of the U302 engine gets 877 hours of work. Other "race horse" engines give only 750 to 833 hours of work for the same 100 million revolutions. This tradition of low rpm and long piston stroke MM engines dates back to the Twin City era.

Standard equipment on the Super models included 12-volt ignition, battery, alternator, starter, ammeter, tachometer, deluxe upholstered wraparound seat, power steering, individual foot brakes, foot clutch, lighting package, Ampli-Torc, rear PTO, Tel-O-Flo hydraulic system, and manually adjustable rear axle.

Under extra equipment, or options, were power adjustable rear wheels, Flote-Ride Seat, high-altitude heads for LP gas or gasoline engines, three-point hitch including lift arms, belt pulley, front-end weights, rear wheel weights, and a bevy of other features.

The gasoline Super model tractors didn't have their own set of serial numbers but continued on from the Model U302 numbering

Built in 1964, this M602 was unusual in that it was fueled by LP gas rather than gasoline or diesel. Its engine makes use of 336 ci to transfer 54 horsepower to the drawbar and 61 horsepower to the PTO, according to Nebraska test results.

with the same prefix of 276. The gasoline Super stayed in the line through 1970.

The first Model U302 Diesel model appeared with the Super tractors in 1967 and continued in production through 1970. This was the same tractor with the same specs, only sporting the D236-4 engine. Factory-observed horsepower was pegged at 44 drawbar and 52 PTO.

A low-production tractor, the Super LP was made in 1969 and 1970 with 25 copies produced each year. It shared all the specs and features of the gasoline Super but rated a bit higher on the horsepower scale. Factory-observed testing gave it 48 on the drawbar and 55 on the PTO.

MM altered its serial numbering system in 1969–1970. The new system separated the LP gas tractor serial numbers from the gasoline tractor numbers. Previously both fuel models were listed together.

MM M602: 1963–1964

The genealogy of the Model M602 included the Model U, 5 Star, and Model M5. The styling has undergone several changes but the engine is the same 336-4 and is used in the gasoline, LP gas, and diesel Model M602 tractors. Ten forward speeds, from 1.6 to 17.2 miles per hour, resulted from the standard 10/2 Ampli-Torc transmission.

This vehicle had styling to match the Jet Star 3 and the Model U302, with Energy Yellow tin work and wheels and Dyna Brown engine and chassis.

Production of gasoline, including LP gas, Model M602 tractors totaled 2,957 units. Copies of the diesel model totaled 1,772 tractors.

MM M604: 1963–1964

Offered with gasoline, LP gas, and diesel engines, the Model M604 was the power-assist four-wheel-drive version of the Model M602. They were made in considerably fewer numbers—gasoline/LP gas totaled 53 tractors while the diesel version tallied 99 vehicles.

MM M670: 1964–1970

When the M602 series bowed out, the M670 stepped in to provide MM with tractors in the 70-plus PTO-horsepower range.

Both the LP gas and gasoline models were Nebraska-tested, with the LP gas version, test 924 in 1965, yielding 64 drawbar and 74 PTO horsepower. Gasoline test, number 925, rated 64 drawbar and 73 PTO horsepower in 1965. The diesel model, test number 926, came in at 64 drawbar and 71 PTO horses.

This tractor was also closely related to the G1000 model, having cylinder blocks, heads, and related parts interchangeable between the two engines.

No, that's not a Brand IHC or Brand MF plow being toted by this 1964 M670 Super tractor. The plow is an MM TW900 two-way spinner plow for throwing soil in the same direction without dead furrows. With 64 horsepower delivered to the drawbar and 73 to the PTO, the tractor has more than enough power to pull the three bottoms.

Basically the M602 series and the M670 were the same tractor except for minor changes in the styling, and the M670's use of hydrostatic power steering as standard equipment. As an option the M670 could be fitted with a heavy-duty wide extendable front axle.

The Supers came along in 1966 with a slight styling change to the front grille. In 1967 the paint scheme was changed to Energy Yellow on the entire tractor, but otherwise it was the same machine. The Supers didn't have their own serial number prefix but simply continued with the Model M670 numbers. The exception is the LP gas models, which, for unknown reasons, received their own separate serial number prefix of 362 during the last year of production, 1970. There were only 75 Super LP gas tractors made with this serial number prefix.

MM G705 & G706: 1962–1965

Using MM's 504-ci six-cylinder engine, these models render over 100 PTO horsepower. Fuel options were limited to LP gas for the 504-6 engine, or diesel, using the D504-6. Gasoline was not available. The engine had a 4 5/8x6-inch bore and stroke and was governed at 1,600 rpm.

The diesel G705 model, tested at Nebraska in test number 835, registered 93 drawbar and 101 PTO horsepower. Test number 833, on the G706 Diesel, pegged the drawbar horsepower at 89 while the PTO rated 101.

The Model G705 was a two-wheel-drive tractor while the Model G706 featured front-wheel assist. Two different makes of front axle were outsourced for the four-wheel-drive tractors. First-production models used the Elwood axle, which was replaced with the Coleman unit on the LP gas models beginning at serial number 24000073. On the diesel models, this change took place at serial number 24100107. The front-wheel assist could be disengaged by a lever on the operator's platform when not needed, or for road travel.

These tractors had only the 5/1 transmission giving forward speeds of 3.3 to 18.3 miles per hour. Cab and air conditioning were available as an option for those who wanted to add even more luxury to the Control Zone Comfort operator's platform.

The Model G705 and Model G706 were manufactured for Massey-Ferguson and carried the designation MF 97 in Massey colors.

Providing more traction through front-wheel assist, the G706 exudes a feeling of power and capability. It was one of the first MM high horsepower tractors to give farmers the advantages of a three-point hitch option, although not internally regulated. Two auxiliary hydraulic cylinders provided positive action both up and down. This 1964 model carried a 504-ci diesel engine that gave 89 drawbar and 101 PTO horsepower verified at Nebraska.

MM G707 & G708: 1965 only

Introduced in June of 1965 as an upgrade of the G705 and G706, these models carried the same 504-ci engine and the same transmission, plus identical horsepower specs.

Changes and improvements are spelled out in a company press release announcing the new tractors. "Minneapolis-Moline will introduce its new Model G-707 2-wheel drive and G-708 4-wheel drive tractors in June, with 101 observed PTO horsepower, new styling, many refinements in the 504 cubic inch engine, and numerous improvements in tractor design. Both will be available for diesel and LP gas.

"New styling of the two tractors embodies the latest design program for Minneapolis-Moline tractors, including wheelbase,

quadruple headlight recessed in the new fenders, new wrap-around company identification, and new three-point hitch."

Also standard was the "free-wheeling" lever to disengage the front-wheel drive on the G708 front-wheel assist. The fuel filtering system was improved and a new dry-type air cleaner was part of the package.

Engine improvements were also spelled out in the press release. "To improve even further the already outstanding performance ratings of this class of tractor and engine, the numerous refinements include: improved sealing characteristics for the cylinder head with added studs and a new combination gasket that employs metal around the combustion chambers and a layer of fiber for oil control; new precision-balanced impeller and sealing in the water pump."

A special option on the two-wheel-drive model was a 14-inch-shorter wheelbase for tighter turning radius when working in restricted areas. Energy Yellow tin work and wheels combined with Dyna Brown engine and chassis was continued from the G705 and G706 models.

As far as we know these didn't make the transformation to Massey-Ferguson products.

MM G900: 1967–1969

This tractor was a row-crop vehicle that pushed the 100 horsepower mark for MM's line, and came with gasoline, LP gas, or diesel engines. Horsepower for the gasoline model, Nebraska test number 980, was 89 drawbar and 97 PTO, while the LP gas tractor, test number 979, registered 86 drawbar and 97 at the PTO. Test number 978 pegged the diesel model horsepower specs as 88 drawbar and 97 PTO horsepower.

Gasoline and LP gas units had the 425C-6 six-cylinder engine with a 4 1/4x5-inch bore and stroke. The diesel model had a slightly larger bore, 4 3/8, with the same stroke. Both engines were governed at 1,800 rpm.

Four front-wheel axle choices were available, which included the standard, two-wheel tricycle, single wheel, or the wide adjustable configuration. The tranny was the 10/2 Ampli-Torc with 10 forward speeds from 2.2 to 17.4 miles per hour.

Until sometime late in 1969, the gasoline and LP gas model serial numbers weren't broken out separately. At this time the LP gas began with its own serial number, 36300001, and ran through 36300160.

The front-wheel-assist version of the G900 Diesel was produced in 1968 with the same engine and specs as the two-wheel-drive model. Of course the front-wheel assist wasn't available with the different front axle options of the other models.

The company's *Product News No. 3-100-4*, dated 4-1-1969, announces a field-installed steel cab for the Model G1000 Vista and the Model G900 tractors. This document lists "year around comfort," convenience, and roomy interior. Specifically the cabs were pressurized and equipped with an air filter that provided 400 cubic feet per minute of clean filtered air. Dome light, heater, windshield wipers, and rearview mirrors were standard.

It wasn't necessary to remove the fenders or lights to install the cab. Apparently air conditioning wasn't available, but the roof was insulated and painted white to reduce radiant heat.

On March 3, 1969, MM's *Product News Letter* announced that a new three-speed Ampli-Torc transmission was available, as an option, for the G1000, G900, and M670. This option remained available through the 50 Series production, which included the G950, G1050, and G1350 tractors.

MM G1000 Row-Crop: 1965–1968

These tractors replaced the G705 and G706 and provided MM with a true "over-100-horsepower" row-crop tractor in gasoline, LP gas, and diesel versions. Engine types were 504A-6 for the gasoline and LP gas models, and D504A-6 for the diesel version.

Will the real tractor please stand up, er, pull ahead? Which is the G706 delivered in 1964 and which is the exacting scale model G706 produced by Roger Mohr and his sons of Vail, Iowa? It requires a second glance to discern which is which.

Both engines were six cylinders with 4 5/8x5-inch bore and stroke governed at 1,800 rpm. Tested at Nebraska, test number 954 in 1966, the LP gas model was rated 99 horsepower at the drawbar and 110 at the PTO. The diesel model, Nebraska test number 953, produced 102 drawbar and 110 PTO horsepower.

The transmission on all models was the 10/2 Ampli-Torc and three front axle choices were available—the two-wheel tricycle, single wheel, or wide adjustable.

A hood and grille styling change occurred on the gasoline and LP gas models at serial number 30500051, and for the diesel model at serial number 30600101. The new look featured an unbroken black stripe around the entire hood.

MM G1000 Wheatland and Rice Special: 1966–1969

These tractors were the replacement for the G707 and G708 models. Basically they shared the same specs as the row-crop mod-els, but were only available with the Standard I-Beam front axle. Standard equipment included hydrostatic power steering, 540 and 1,000 rpm PTO, and two 12-volt batteries.

A field-installed cab was an option. No doubt they were also available with the front-wheel-assist package although the serial number list doesn't break these models out into separate numbers. Another thing that remains unclear is whether any gasoline tractors were actually produced. The serial number prefix list included a gasoline model along with the LP gas.

During production these tractors were redesigned with heavier gearing and the paint scheme was changed to all Energy Yellow. This took place, in the LP gas models, at serial number 32600576. The diesel model change came at serial number 32700926.

A few conventional row-crop tractors also received the same modification and redesign, but the serial numbers for this change weren't noted.

Too young and capable yet to retire, this G1000 Vista makes good use of its 504-ci engine to edge above the 100 horsepower level. It puts out 102 drawbar horsepower and 111 PTO horsepower. This tractor reflected MM's improved operator comfort in the G1000 series advertised as "Control Zone Comfort." According to the owner of this 1969 model, "Visibility is terrific." The front-wheel-assist Vista is a rare tractor with low production numbers.

MM G1000 Vista: 1967–1969

"Vista" could be interpreted as "Super." It was an upgrade of the Model G1000, but the engine and specs remained the same. What did change was the paint scheme, which discontinued the Dyna Brown engine and chassis, leaving an all-Energy Yellow vehicle, including the wheels.

The fuel tank was relocated to behind the operator's platform and increased in capacity from 39 gallons to 42 gallons for LP gas and from 40 gallons to 56 gallons for diesel.

Introduced in 1968, the front-wheel-assist G1000 Vista Diesel joined the line and stayed through 1969. It was the same tractor except for the front axle configuration. What we don't know is the number actually produced. The serial number list accounts for only 1968 production and these numbers fall within the Model G1000 Diesel serial numbers.

Actual tractors do exist with numbers higher than those listed. The highest serial number we are aware of is 34601553. An experimental Model G1000 Vista has survived and carries serial number X635.

MM Jet Star 2: 1963 Only

With the exception of the paint scheme and the diesel engine injection pump, the change from Jet Star to Jet Star 2 didn't affect the basic engine and transmission specifications.

The all-metallic bronze paint scheme of the Jet Star gave way to Energy Yellow tin work and wheels and Dyna Brown engine and chassis.

The Bosch injection pump on the diesel Jet Star was switched to the Roosa-Master on the Jet Star 2 tractors.

The Jet Star 2 Series was offered in gasoline, LP gas, and diesel for all models including Orchard tractors.

MM Jet Star 3 & Jet Star 3 Super: 1964–1970

All of the Jet Star 3 and Jet Star 3 Super tractors used the 206-ci engine with a 3 5/8x5-inch bore and stroke and had the 10/2 Ampli-Torc transmission.

Factory-observed horsepower was listed as follows: gasoline, drawbar 39 and PTO 44; LP gas, drawbar 40 and PTO 45; diesel, drawbar 36 and PTO 40. This is a good example to show that factory-observed ratings and Nebraska ratings were very close in many instances. Nebraska test number 789 for the gasoline Jet Star 3 placed the drawbar horsepower at 39 and the PTO at 44, which is exactly the same as the factory numbers. For the LP gas model, Nebraska test number 790 put the horsepower at 41 on the drawbar and 45 at the PTO.

The customer could choose any of the four front-wheel options—standard, single wheel, two-wheel tricycle, or wide adjustable.

Company advertisements said, "The Jet Star Series could be bought stripped down or fully equipped according to your needs."

Production of the Jet Star 3 gasoline and LP gas ran from 1964 through 1965. The diesel model Jet Star 3 and Super ran from 1964 through 1970.

In 1965 the Jet Star 3 Super gasoline and LP gas came aboard and ran through 1970. Actually in 1970 there were 10 Super LP gas models broken out into their own serial numbers.

From 1965 through 1967, the Jet Star 3 Orchard/Super Orchard model in LP gas was offered while the Jet Star 3 Super Orchard in diesel was a 1967-only offering.

The Orchard models had independent PTO, engine side enclosures, complete rear fender cowling, and heavy front axle, but no hydraulics. With the 10/2 Ampli-Torc tranny, the forward speed ranged from 1.5 to 15.8 miles per hour.

A gasoline Industrial model was made in both 1966 and 1967, while the diesel Industrial was a 1966-only production vehicle.

The Jet Star 3 was manufactured as the Cockshutt 1350 from 1966 through 1968 with its own set of Cockshutt serial numbers. Except for the tin work and color scheme, it was the same tractor as the MM model.

Many decades after it came off the assembly line in 1966, this Jet Star 3 Super is still routinely doing its job in the field. It puts out 41 horsepower at the drawbar and 44 horsepower at the PTO from an engine of just 206 ci.

It might look a real hand-built prototype of an M6 tractor, but only the hand-built is correct. This is a proof-of-concept scale model completed in 1963. Since White purchased Motec in 1963 this is possibly the last prototype built under the Motec name. *Roger Mohr Collection*

Sporting a six-cylinder engine rigged for LP gas, this G1050 had 99 drawbar horsepower from a 504-ci engine. The diesel model barely cleared the 100-horsepower barrier with 101 drawbar horsepower from a diesel version of the 504-ci engine.

MINNEAPOLIS-MOLINE TRACTORS BOW OUT

The Model G350 and Model G450 tractors were completely Fiat-built units made in Turin, Italy, then shipped to Decatur, Georgia, where they were painted either MM colors or Oliver colors. This changed in 1975 when the entry point for these units became Canada, where they were assembled, painted, and processed. Production records are inconclusive concerning years manufactured, serial numbers, and numbers produced. We will give the best information that we have at this writing. Since these tractors were built in Italy and processed in the United States on a "demand only" basis, it's possible that they could have appeared in company advertisements for an unknown time before any were actually sold. It is almost certain that the serial numbers were kept under the Oliver name and production records.

The Oliver Model 1265 was the same tractor as the MM Model G350, while the Oliver Model 1365 and MM Model G450 were the same with appropriate tin and paint. White also sold these tractors with its tin and paint as the Model 1270 and Model 1370.

These MM tractors appear in Larsen's *Farm Tractors 1950-1975* under the year 1971, but no tests were conducted.

MM G350/G450: 1971–1975

Production records are based on the Oliver model production of these tractors, which isn't a guarantee that MM G350 and G450 models were made during each of these years.

Company advertising touted these models as "The new Mini-Models. Spirited combination of work-horse and chore-pony."

Both tractors used a diesel engine with 3.94x4.33-inch bore and stroke governed at 2,400 rpm. The Model G350 had a three-cylinder engine with 158 ci, while the Model G450 added one more cylinder, giving a displacement of 210 ci. Factory-estimated PTO horsepower was 41 for the Model G350 and 54 for the Model G450.

Available in Utility and four-wheel-drive models, the Model G350 had a fixed front tread of 56 1/4 or 65 inches and rear tread adjustment comparable to the Utility model.

The G450 offered a row-crop model with 25 inches of ground clearance, plus the Utility and four-wheel-drive versions. Another feature was wide adjustment in tread width and the option of power-adjust rims. Both the Model G350 and Model G450 front-wheel assist could be disengaged when not needed.

Transmissions are best explained by this quote from the ad brochure: "The G350 gives you a choice of six forward speeds—selected with a single gearshift lever. And, the dual-range transmission in the G450 enables you to crawl along at 4/10 mph (1970 rpm with optional creeper gears) or hit a lively clip of 15 mph. You get eight forward speeds with a standard transmission, 12 forward with creeper gears."

Both tractors are equipped with PTO, power steering, 12-volt electrical system, and three-point hitch.

Both the Model G550 and Model G750 used an Oliver-built six-cylinder engine wound a little tighter than the MM engines with the governed rpm at 2,200. The Model G550 was bored and stroked at 3 5/8x3 3/4 inches; the Model G750 at 3 3/4x4 inches.

The Oliver models were tested at Nebraska, which presumably would produce identical numbers for their MM counterparts. Test number 943 placed the Oliver 1550 Diesel, MM Model G550, at 45 drawbar and 53 PTO horsepower. The gasoline tractor, test number 944, rated 53 PTO horsepower. The LP gas version wasn't tested but was certified by Oliver as 51 horsepower at the PTO.

Test number 1041 at Nebraska for the Oliver 1655 Diesel, MM Model G750, resulted in 61 drawbar and 70 PTO horses, while the gasoline version rated 70 at the PTO.

Standard transmission for both models was a 6/2 that could be upgraded to a Hydra-Power Drive giving 12 forward speeds for the Model G550. The optional Hydraul-Shift was available on the Model G750 giving 18 forward speeds.

Other optional and special equipment included Powerjuster rear wheels, rear wheel weights, and front frame weights. Fender, or wheel guard, fuel tanks were listed for the Model G750 increasing the fuel capacity from 27 1/2 to 105 1/2 gallons. Also under the options were an anti-roll bar with canopy and seat belt, and a cab with heater. Tilt-O-Scope power steering, three-point hitch, and single or dual speed PTO rounded out the package.

Wide adjustable, utility, and tricycle front axle were available for the Model G550 and also for the Model G750 which, in addition, offered a front-wheel-assist model with an optional "no spin" differential.

There was one Model G750 prototype built by MM and this tractor is still in existence.

MM G940: 1971 only

This tractor was an Oliver-built product flying the MM grille and colors. It's the same vehicle as the Oliver Model 1855 with a turbocharged 310-ci six-cylinder engine in either gasoline or diesel fuel. Bore and stroke measured 3 7/8x4 3/8 inches on the diesel model and the governed engine speed was 2,400 rpm. Bore and stroke on the gasoline engine was 3 7/8x4 inches. Factory tests estimated

Thanks to specially commissioned artwork that led the prospective buyer's gaze directly to the tractor, he couldn't help but be impressed with the styling of the G350 and G450. These tractors were built in Italy by Fiat and shipped to Decatur, Georgia, for painting, tires, and distribution to U.S. dealerships. *Cal Overlee Collection*

Energy Yellow was the dominant color for these MM tractors set off by white wheels, white grille, and white hood stripe for name and model identification. The grille styling was unique to the Model G350 and Model G450.

MM G550/G750: 1971 Only

Built by Oliver at the Charles City plant, the MM Model G550 and Oliver Model 1555 were twins except for the grille and paint. The same applies to the MM Model G750 and the Oliver 1655. Not only were they built by Oliver, they contained all Oliver components.

Although the company literature lists only gasoline and diesel models, the Oliver tractors were also available in an LP gas version so customers could probably get the MM in LP gas as well, if they asked.

PTO horsepower at 98 diesel and 92 gasoline.

The Model G940 was available in wide adjustable row-crop, Wheatland/Ricefield, and power-assist front axle.

The Hydraul-Shift transmission provided three speeds in each of the six forward gears, dependent on the operator's choice of underdrive, direct drive, or overdrive range.

MM's Comfort Zone raised platform provided "wander-free" power steering and a telescoping tilt steering wheel column adjustable into four positions for sitting or standing.

Some options were Poweradjust rear wheels, category III hitch, wide-swinging drawbar without three-point hitch, wheel guard fuel tanks, roll bar with canopy and seat belt, and a factory-installed cab with air conditioner.

MM G850: 1971 only

Another Oliver-built tractor, the MM Model G850 is the same unit as the Oliver Model 1755 and virtually identical to the MM Model G940 in standard and extra equipment. The factory estimate for PTO horsepower was 86 for both the gasoline and diesel models.

MM G950: 1969–1972

Roles were reversed with the MM Model G950 and Oliver Model 1865. This time it was MM building the tractor and Oliver putting its grille and colors on the tractor.

The six-cylinder engine was an MM-built 425C-6 in LP gas and D451-6 in diesel. A two- or three-speed Ampli-Torc was available on the transmission as an option but a closed-center hydraulic system was standard on row-crop models. The Model G950 delivered 97 PTO horsepower and was available in standard tread and row-crop front axle.

The LP gas model's last year was 1971, but the diesel tractor ran through 1972. The grille featured the large "White" lettering on the front.

MM G1050: 1969–1972

Built at the Lake Street plant in Minneapolis, Minnesota, the MM Model G1050 and Oliver Model 2055 came from the same spec sheet except for the paint and grille. Fitted with the 504-ci diesel or LP gas naturally aspirated engine, these models developed 110 PTO horsepower according to the

The G750 was designed to be sort of a utility infielder for middle-sized farms—it could be used in the field for the pulling jobs or be equally as comfortable doing work around the farmyard. *Cal Overlee Collection*

manufacturer. Row-crop and Standard models were the only front axle choices available. The three-speed Ampli-Torc drive allowed a speed range from 1.67 to 19.26 miles per hour. Closed center hydraulics provided full draft control on the three-point hitch system.

The Model G1050 styling also featured the large "WHITE" lettering on the grille, Energy Yellow tin work and chassis, and white wheels.

MM G1350: 1969–1972

Oliver's Model 2155 and MM's Model G1350 are the same tractor under appropriate paint and grille design.

The LP gas engine was the MM-built 504B-6, and the diesel the MM-built D585-6. Previous to this engine, MM used the Lanova injection system for its diesel engines. With the Model G1350 this was changed to a direct injection system.

The G850 with 86 PTO horsepower and the G940 with 98 horsepower were marketed as combining the necessary power with convenience of operation and operator comfort. *Cal Overlee Collection*

MINNEAPOLIS-MOLINE. MM

Built to make your farm future more productive

Models G850/G940

Nebraska test number 1069, conducted in 1971, rated the diesel model at 125 drawbar and 141 PTO horsepower.

A nice feature of these machines was a computer-controlled three-point hitch with upper and lower link sensing for Category II– and Category III–mounted equipment. Rear wheels were adjustable from 61 to 84 inches and front axle options were wide adjustable and Standard I-Beam. The tractor was available with a customized factory cab.

The 1971 and 1972 models of the G950, G1050, and G1350 received a grille design change. The early models had a long fiberglass nose piece on the grille with "WHITE" lettering. The later tractors had a flatter grille design framed with cast iron. This style reverted back to the "MM" lettering.

Five prototypes of a Wheatland LP gas model were built in 1969 and looked a lot like the Model G1000 Wheatland.

Breaking with tradition, the 1969 Heritage model G950 was available with patriotic red, white, and blue paint schemes. The G950 was an all MM product. It has 87 drawbar horsepower from 425 ci in the LP gas version and 88 drawbar horsepower from 451 ci in diesel format.

MM's Articulated Four-Wheel-Drive Tractor

MM's first entry into the articulated four-wheel-drive arena was the A4T-1400. The development of this tractor is interesting enough to warrant some in-depth coverage.

The following information is taken from a paper presented before the Society of Automotive Engineers, "Development of White Farm Equipment's Articulated Four-Wheel-Drive Tractor," by R. H. Lytle, M. J. Verhulst, and R. O. Westra. The paper was presented September 14–17, 1970.

The need for high-horsepower farm tractors was well established, so the challenge facing the engineering staff at White was how to provide a well-engineered vehicle at an economical price, and how to move it to the marketplace quickly.

We'll deal with the three challenges in reverse order. First challenge—how to get it to market quickly.

Before you can say something is accomplished quickly you need to know what is considered normal for that particular task. Normally the design of a new agricultural vehicle would take years. The John Deere New Generation tractors took seven years from inception to final production. Modification of an existing model can require one to two years.

The schedule that White adopted for the A4T vehicle was eight months. Hopeful? Yes. Ambitious? Certainly. Unrealistic? Incredibly, it proved not to be. The schedule called for a running prototype by May 15, 1969. Work from a rough sketch started in early March of 1969 and on May 16,

The Stuttgart Tractors

During the 1950s the horsepower race for bigger tractors was in full swing. In the early 1950s Wagner introduced its four-wheel-drive agricultural tractor. The Steiger brothers "barn-built" their first four-wheel drive in 1957, and Deere & Company awed customers with its 8010 in 1959. This trend caught the attention of the Prairie Implement Company of Stuttgart, Arkansas.

Sometime in the early 1950s, Don Oliver, a partner in Prairie Implement; Gale Stroh, the company's sales manager; and shop foreman, Kenneth Bull, decided to design, and build, their own articulated four-wheel-drive tractor. The resulting "Stuttgart tractors" were part of this historic trend toward today's mega-horsepower tractors.

During an interview, Oliver recalled how the Stuttgart was developed:

"Company sales manager Gale Stroh thought we should do something about a bigger tractor, because farmers were beginning to want to farm larger acres. We went to look at some industrial units, M-R-S, and other brands.

At that time we were trading for a lot of used tractors and there wasn't a lot of market for them. So we decided to start building [four-wheel-drive models] out of used tractors, using the two final drives. The first one was built out of a couple of Minneapolis-Moline Model U tractors. However, they proved too narrow, because by the time we got the power unit up on the front they were kind of high and they wanted to turn over. Next we tried the Model G and Model GVI."

Things progressed even further when Stroh was at the MM factory, sometime in 1959, where he saw a running gear and drive train MM had developed for an industrial gravel spreader. Stroh believed these units would work quite well on the articulated tractors they were experimenting with in Stuttgart. After some explanation and negotiation, Stroh convinced MM to provide running gear, drive train, and a power unit to the Stuttgart project. The articulated tractor that resulted was purchased by Oliver for use in his farming operation.

This tractor was built during 1960 and delivered to the Oliver farm January 1, 1961, where it did farm work for the next eight years. During the winter of 1969 it was put back in the shop and redesigned. Oliver explained, "My son and I did the redesign on my tractor in 1969. We lowered the platform, tapered the front end, put a different ladder on it. We put a white band with black letters around the hood like MM was using on its newer, later tractors."

About this time, Oliver's Stuttgart tractor attracted the interest of management at MM. Oliver remembers a phone call he received:

"Vice President Don Cox called and wanted to know if he could bring a carload of people to look at my tractor. This was in February. When the day was over, Cox asked if they could take the tractor to Minneapolis.

It was about time to start field work so I asked for the tractor to be back by March 1. It was, and on May 15 he called and said, 'We want you up here, the plane ticket's on MM.' When I got up there they already had the first A4T prototype built. It didn't look like my tractor (different tin work) but they copied the steering and frame work off my tractor. They put a diesel engine on it and called it the A4T-1400.

It was already tested; they didn't have to do anything and MM now had the first economical four-wheel-drive agricultural tractor on the market."

A total of 34 Stuttgart tractors were built at the Prairie Implement dealership. The majority used LP gas powerplants, but if a customer preferred diesel they installed a Cummins engine.

With the exception of Oliver's tractor, all other Stuttgart units were built with used components. Unfortunately, there weren't any Stuttgart serial numbers applied to the tractors although Oliver's tractor does have an interesting story concerning serial numbers. Oliver said, "The tractor I have has a serial number on the engine and it is serial number 1. It isn't the first 605 engine they made, but it must have been the first HD 605 they produced. My tractor has an LP gas engine and we never tested for horsepower; it doesn't have a PTO, but the engine is rated something over 100 horsepower."

Today Oliver maintains a MM Museum where his Stuttgart tractor is a star attraction.

---

an unpainted, but running, first prototype was completed.

While the first prototype was being built, any changes that were warranted were recorded and sent to the drafting department to document the required specification from which new parts were fabricated for the second prototype. This second unit verified the new specifications and then all new drawings and specs were released to the manufacturing department, allowing it to begin preparation for production scheduling. This accelerated program worked so well that few changes were required and production began in November of 1969—right on schedule, eight months later.

The second challenge, how to produce it economically, is closely tied to the first challenge. Other agricultural tractor manufacturers had discovered that articulated four-wheel-drive tractors built from outsourced components proved too costly to be marketed effectively. Again, Deere & Company's 8010 is an example. Just as unacceptable was tooling up to manufacture a unit that would have relatively low sales numbers.

The A4T-1600 offered several engine options providing power ranging from 169 to 225 horsepower from displacements between 504 and 800-ci. It had ten forward and two reverse speeds, fuel tank capacities up to 104 gallons, and unfueled and unballasted weight of 17,300 pounds. An A4T-1400 was also available at 139 horsepower.

White solved the dilemma, as did other companies, by designing the vehicle around existing high-volume in-house components.

The initial selection for an engine was the MM D504A-6, the same diesel power plant used in the MM Model G1050 two-wheel-drive tractor. For the LP gas version they chose the new MM 504B-6 engine, developed for use in the MM Model G1350 tractor.

The best choice for a suitable transmission was the 5/1 used in the MM Model G1350, minus the underdrive feature. By placing a two-speed transfer case behind the transmission, the A4T was equipped with 10 forward ground speeds.

Axle size hinged on the requirement that each axle be capable of taking at least two-thirds of the engine power. The axles used in the MM Model G950 met these specifications. Using existing MM conventional two-wheel-drive tractor axles allowed adjustable wheel treads from 76 to 96 inches with "off-the-shelf" agricultural tires. This also meant that standard production duals for conventional two-wheel-drive tractors could be mounted on the A4T.

The brake components were the same as those used on the MM Model G1350 and were standard on the rear axle. For extreme conditions they could also be fitted to the front axle.

112

Two types of hydraulic systems were offered for this articulated tractor. Standard equipment was an open-center system with two valves for remote cylinders, while a closed-center system for three-point hitch and up to three remote cylinders was offered as an option. Many of the parts were common to the hydraulic systems on existing production tractors. Other standard two-wheel-drive tractor parts utilized in the A4T production include the radiator, air cleaner, grille, engine sheet metal, steering support, electrical system, instrument panel, platform, seat, clutch pedal, brake pedal, transmission controls, and throttle controls.

Items that required new design and production were an articulating frame, transfer case, a rear platform wrapper, hydraulic control console, and fenders. In keeping with the goal of rapid development and cost control, for any application where an existing part couldn't be used, MM engineers and machinists modified the one that came closest rather than developing an entirely new part.

The cab was one exception to this rule. A noise level goal of 86 dB was set, and an entirely new modular cab design was created, meeting the standard.

The third challenge, a well-engineered vehicle, was met by bending the traditional

rules of designing and engineering a new product. As the authors explained, MM used a task force approach that included just one man from the working staff of each major operating group within the company. This project was given top priority and the "force" was allowed to cut through any unnecessary paperwork, relying on verbal authorization to expedite production coupled with minimum micromanagement. Bottom line is, it worked and the A4T-1400 and A4T-1600 are examples of the success.

An interesting footnote to the story involves a field installation of a larger engine. To quote from the above-mentioned paper, "We are watching with considerable interest some developments in our Peoria branch area, where 20 or more A4T tractors have had their engines exchanged for MM 800 cu in. LP power unit engines by some 'Maverick' dealers and customers. It will be interesting to see if they can obtain total utilization of this available horsepower."

MM A4T-1400: 1969–1970

First models were powered by MM's D504A-6 diesel engine with 4 5/8x5-inch bore and stroke. The 1,800-rpm naturally aspirated engine delivered 139 factory observed horsepower. Slap on a turbocharger and it kicked the horsepower to 151.

MM's long-serving 5/1 transmission was mated to a two-speed transfer case that effectively provided 10 forward speeds from 1 to 18.2 miles per hour.

Outsourced cabs were available for first-production tractors but soon MM began producing its own cab. This was the first self-contained, rubber-mounted pod unit offered on a farm tractor. The company hailed them as the "Quietest cab on any tractor."

This same tractor in Oliver trappings was the Model 2455.

MM A4T-1600: 1970–1972

The next generation of MM's articulated four-wheel drive took the same concept to another horsepower level with a diesel as well as LP gas engine. Oliver marketed this tractor as its Model 2655.

The LP gas model used the 504B-6 MM-made six-cylinder engine with a 4 5/8x5-inch bore and stroke cranked up to 2,200 rpm delivering 169 factory observed horsepower. The diesel version had more cubic-inch displacement from the D585-6 six-cylinder, yet naturally aspirated, and at the same rpm, it generated the same 169 factory observed horsepower. Nebraska got different results for the A4T-1600 in 1971, test number 1070, recording 129 drawbar and 143 PTO horsepower.

Diesel fuel tank capacity is 104 gallons and the LP gas model tank holds 90 gallons at 80 percent full. The A4T-1600 had the same transmission setup as the A4T-1400 with a forward speed range of 2 to 22.2 miles per hour.

The A4T-1400 and A4T-1600 would articulate 44 degrees in either direction and oscillate 15 degrees in either direction, which kept four wheels on the ground even in the roughest terrain.

These units could turn in a 15-foot radius, weighed approximately 17,300 pounds, and cost $12,000 to $15,000. In a departure from MM's long time color scheme, the A4T tractors came painted red, white, and black. The exception was the Plainsman with Heritage colors of red, white, and blue. The Heritage colors also included five blue stars on the rear fender.

At the left are two Heritage models in red, white, and blue and at the right a standard production A4T-1600. From the left: A4T-1600 Plainsman, G950, and A4T-1600. Drawbar horsepower is, respectively, 190, 86, and 128. This image shows the "WHITE" on the grille of early models and the "MM" on the grille of later tractors.

The Last Two Minneapolis-Moline Models

Slowly but surely, White's management began to integrate the Oliver and MM line into a hybrid tractor with components from both lines, married to new tin work.

The period between 1973 and 1974 saw Oliver's influence overshadow the MM tractors, and by the end of 1974 the MM line no longer existed.

MM tractors manufactured during 1973 and 1974 were built in Charles City, Iowa, using an Oliver drivetrain and MM engines.

MM G955: 1973–1974

Developed as the replacement for the Model G950, this tractor was painted Energy Yellow with contrasting white wheels and grille. The engine was the same MM-built power plant as the G950, but it was coupled to an Oliver drivetrain in the G955 model. A diesel model G955 was tested at Nebraska in 1974, test number 1161, which yielded 83 drawbar and 98 PTO horsepower.

With the White badge, tin, and red paint it became the White Model 1870. It

was targeted at the Canadian market but actually ended up being exported to more countries than just Canada.

Early G955 and G1355 models had the white band on the sides of the hood and "MM" in the upper grille. The later models had all yellow hood sides and "WHITE" in the upper grille area.

MM G1355: 1973–1974

This tractor is another joint effort between MM and Oliver—MM engine, LP gas or diesel, and Oliver drivetrain from the clutch back, with over-and-under Hydraul-Shift providing 18 forward speeds.

The six-cylinder diesel engine displaced 585 ci while the LP gas version displaced 504 ci. Test number 1141, in 1973, at Nebraska pegged the horsepower as 128 drawbar and 142 PTO.

The heavy-duty lower-link sensitivity three-point hitch accommodates Category II and Category III implements and can lift a hefty 6,000 pounds. The closed-center hydraulic system supplies full-time power steering, triple-disc brakes, remote cylinders, and PTO clutch.

The cab is built around a rollover protective structure and isolated from the frame with rubber blocks to absorb shocks, vibrations, and noise. Optional features on the cab include air conditioning, heater, radio, and side-saddle diesel fuel tanks.

The White version, with appropriate tin work and red paint, was marketed in Canada as the Model 2270. The G955 and G1355 were also sold with Oliver badges and the Oliver green paint scheme.

The G955 and G1355 were the last of the tractors to carry the proud MM badge.

Closing the Door on Minneapolis-Moline

Just how and when the decision was made to discontinue the MM line is uncertain, though company correspondence and press releases show some of the relevant corporate restructuring and decisions. A big factor in the decision was the troubled economic conditions down on the farm.

On August 1, 1972, White Motor Corporation Corporate Director of Industrial Relations Thomas J. Naglieri testified in federal district court in Minnesota in a lawsuit

With 97 horsepower in the diesel model, and five less in the gasoline and LP engine versions, the G955 was just barely under the magic 100 horsepower mark. *Dennis Parker collection*

"Tractors manufactured at the Lake Street plant have carried the brand label 'Minneapolis-Moline.' Minneapolis-Moline tractors, we believe, are high quality products. However, Minneapolis-Moline tractors have always had only a small segment of the tractor market, as compared with giants such as John Deere, International Harvester, and Ford tractors. When business conditions become depressed, the small manufacturer has an even more difficult time competing with the giants.

"During 1970 and 1971, the losses experienced in the operation of the Lake Street and Hopkins plants aggregate $15,061,145."

The losses the company was suffering help explain some of its many restructuring decisions. On February 11, 1970, White Farm Equipment had issued a news release from offices at Hopkins, Minnesota. In part it said, "The farm equipment operations of White Motor Corporation, Cleveland, have been consolidated with new headquarters at Hopkins, Minnesota. The previous White farm equipment subsidiaries, Oliver Corporation, Chicago; Minneapolis-Moline, Inc., Hopkins; and Cockshutt Farm Equipment Company Limited, Brantford (Ontario), have been merged into a newly-named subsidiary, White Farm Equipment Company."

Then on December 22, 1970, another *News Bulletin* was issued from Cleveland, Ohio, which said, in part, "H. J. Nave, President of White Motor Corporation, today announced a new organizational structure for White's farm equipment companies. These include Oliver Corporation, Charles City, Iowa; Minneapolis-Moline, Inc., Hopkins, Minnesota; and Oliver's Implement Plant, South Bend, Indiana. Nave stated that the new structure would better serve the needs of the individual farmer and the respective dealers of each company. Under the new structure, Oliver, Minneapolis-Moline and South Bend Implements will be organized as completely separate operating companies with headquarters at their manufacturing plant locations."

Additional changes were spelled out in an interoffice letter of May 26, 1972, from the White Motor Corporation to all White Farm Equipment dealers in the United States and Canada. The letter declared, "On January 3, 1972, White announced a restructuring of the farm equipment division which

against the company by union workers. The case was International Union, United Automobile, Aerospace and Agricultural Implement Workers of America—UAW, and its local union Nos. 932, 1147, 107, and 337, vs. White Motor Corporation and White Farm Equipment Company, its wholly owned subsidiary. Naglieri testified:

"During the late 1960s, and continuing to the present time, the farm equipment business

has been severely depressed nationally. This has been particularly true in connection with the manufacture and sale of tractors. The trend in agriculture has been toward larger farming units, as a consequence of which farmers purchase larger and more powerful tractors and bigger farm implements. For tractor manufacturers, this has meant fewer and larger units are sold, with a resulting decline in dollar sales and units produced.

This is a good angle to appreciate the high, roomy Control Zone Comfort operator's platform. It also shows the fender fuel tanks and front-end weight system. These features along with plenty of horsepower made the G1355 a good seller for the company. *Floyd County Historical Museum*

included the phasing out of operations at both Lake Street and Hopkins, Minnesota, in June of 1972.

"As you know, manufacturing, engineering, research, development and marketing staffs have already been consolidated."

Specifically, the following five steps of the new program were listed:

1. We are now transferring to Charles City the production of Minneapolis-Moline parts, certain tractor engines and the Minneapolis-Moline line of power units.

2. Two Minneapolis-Moline engines will be integrated into production at Charles City. They are the 425 and 585 cubic inch current Minneapolis-Moline diesel and LP gas engines.

3. In addition to new Oliver equipment which will be introduced in the fall of 1972, two new Minneapolis-Moline tractors, 97 and 135 horsepower, will be introduced. The Minneapolis-Moline units will use these current Minneapolis-Moline diesel and LP gas engines exclusively.

4. At the phase-out of the operations at Lake Street and Hopkins in June, we will have ample units of the articulated tractor (A4T) in inventory. We will, however, build that unit in the future at Charles City for as long as there is a substantial demand for this tractor in the marketplace.

5. To support this program, improvements will be made in the foundry to increase its utilization. Added safety and pollution equipment will also be installed.

The future for MM appeared brighter when employment at the Charles City plant rose from 1,200 in October 1972 to 1,850 in March 1973, an increase of 54 percent. Part of this was credited to the excellent market acceptance of the company's new high-horsepower tractors introduced in 1972.

But, for MM, it just wasn't good enough, soon enough.

Later production G955 and G1355 tractors featured the "WHITE" name in the grille instead of MM. Some earlier MM tractors also featured the "WHITE" name but for a time it was changed back to MM when dealers and customers insisted that they wanted only MM tractors. *Floyd County Historical Museum*

Appendix:
Minneapolis-Moline Serial Numbers

Following are all the available serial numbers for all tractors made by firms that came under the banner of the Minneapolis-Moline Power Implement Company.

This list has been compiled from the best information available; however, the records for some models are nonexistent, for some they are incomplete, and all require judicious interpretation of the records and notes.

All numbers are inclusive and if a year isn't listed it means there were no tractors produced for that year, or the serial numbers for that year haven't been preserved.

Moline Plow Company

Year	Start	End	Total
Universal 1914–1915			
	N/A	N/A	N/A

Moline Universal 1915–1917

	N/A	N/A	N/A

Moline Universal D 1917–1923

	N/A*	N/A*	N/A*

*No production records or serial numbers are available. However, a Universal D was tested at Nebraska, test number 33, in July 1920 and that tractor carried serial number 28268.

Moline Orchard Tractor

	N/A	N/A	N/A

Moline Road Tractor

	N/A	N/A	N/A

Minneapolis Threshing Machine Company

MTM serial numbers were in sequence from the first serial number they used for tractors on through production regardless of what model happened to exit the assembly line.

Year	Start	End	Total
MTM 25-50: 1911-1914*			
1911	N/A	N/A	25
1912	N/A	N/A	48
1913	N/A	N/A	N/A
1914	N/A	N/A	N/A

*Built by Northwest Thresher Company

MTM Universal 20-40: 1911–1914*

	N/A	N/A	N/A

*Built by Universal Tractor Company

MTM 40-80: 1912–1920

	N/A	N/A	N/A

MTM 35-70: 1920–1929

	N/A	N/A	N/A

MTM 20-40: 1916–1919

	N/A	N/A	N/A

MTM 22-44: 1920–1927

	N/A	N/A	N/A

MTM 15 & 15-30: 1915–1919

	N/A	N/A	N/A

MTM 12-25: 1919–1926

	N/A	N/A	N/A

MTM 17-30: 1921–1926

	N/A	N/A	N/A

MTM 17-30A: 1926–1934

	N/A	N/A	N/A

MTM 17-30B: 1926–1934

	N/A	N/A	N/A

MTM 27-42: 1929–N/A

	N/A	N/A	N/A

MTM 39-57 & 30-50: 1928–1929

	9550*	10681	N/A

*These are not presented as the only copies made.

Minneapolis Steel and Machinery Company

Year	Start	End	Total
Joy-McVicker 50-140: 1911 only			
1911 only	N/A	N/A	5

TC 40-65A*: 1910–1924

1910–1915	N/A	N/A	N/A
1916–1924	1001	1820	820**

*40-65 with 7 1/4x9-inch bore and stroke
**TC 60-90: 1914–1921 are believed to fall within these serial numbers

TC 40-65B*

	1821	1825	5

*40-65 with 7 3/4x9-inch bore and stroke

TC 25-45: 1913–1920

Model A	2501	2646	146
Model B	2647	2673	27
Model C	2701	2797	97
Model D	2801	2815	15
Model E	2816	3126	311

TC 15-30: 1913–1917

	5001	5478	478

Twentieth Century: 1914–N/A

	N/A	N/A	N/A

TC 16-30: 1917–1920

1917	5501	6203	703
1918	6204	6503	300
1919-1920	N/A	N/A	N/A

Year	Start	End	Total
TC 12-20: 1919–1926			
1919-1926	10201	19903	9,703

TC 20-35: 1920–1926

1920-1926	3201	4097	897

Transitional Models—Twin City and Minneapolis-Moline
TC 17-28 TY: 1926–1935

Pre-1930	20001	30103	10,103
1930	30104	30281	178
1931	30282	30298	17
1932	30299	30309	11
1933	30310	30333	24
1934	30334	30762	429
1935	30763	30808	46

TC 17-28 Industrial: 1934 only

1934	43001	N/A	N/A

TC 27-44 AT: 1926–1935

1926-1928—may fall within TC 20-35 serial numbers			
1929	250001	250730	730
1930	250731	250796	66
1931	250797	250799	3
1934	250800	250805	6
1935	250806	250839	34

TC 21-32: 1926–1928

	150001	150302	302

TC 21-32 FT: 1929–1934

Pre-1930	150303	151796	1,494
1930	151797	154073	2,277
1931	154074	154123	50
1932	154124	154129	6
1934	154130	154275	146

TC 21-32 FTA: 1935–1938

1935	154300	155381	1,082
1936	155382	156247	866
1937	156248	156908	661
1938	156909	157229	321

TC FT Industrial: 1932–1934

1932	46001	46004	4
1934	46005	46029	25

TC FTA Industrial: 1935–1937

1935	46030	only	1
1936	46031	46046	16
1937	46047	46074	28

TC KT: 1929–1934

1929	300001	300079	79
1930	300080	301583	1,504
1931	301584	301862	279
	301865	301866	2
	301882	only	

Year	Start	End	Total
TC KT: 1929–1934 (continued)			
	301891	301956	66
1932	301957	301981	25
1933	301982	301987	6
1934	301988	302078	91
TC KT Orchard			
1931	301863	301864	2
	301867	301881	15
	301883	301890	8
TC KT Industrial: 1932–1935			
1932	40001	only	1
1933	40002	40004	3
1934	40005	40008	4
1935	40009	only	1
TC KTA: 1934–1938			
1934	302200	302371	172
1935	302372	303835	1,464
1936	303826	304701	876
1937	304702	306281	1,580
1938	306282	306751	450
TC Universal MT: 1930–1934			
Pre-1931	525001	525020	20
1931	525021	525095	75
1932	525096	525334	239
1933	525335	525345	11
1934	525346	525420	75
TC Universal MTA: 1934–1938			
1934	525421	525490	70
1935	525491	526118	628
1936	526119	526960	842
1937	526961	528049	1,089
1938	528050	528645	596
TC Universal JT: 1934–1937			
1934	550001	550025	25*
1935	550026	551762	1,737
1936	551763	554554	2,792
1937	554555	556244	1,690

*First 25 units were prototypes—see text for details.

Year	Start	End	Total
TC JT Standard: 1936–1937			
1936	600001	600322	322
1937	600323	600469	147
TC JT Orchard: 1936–1937			
1935	X108	experimental	1
1936	625001	625103	103
1937	625104	625156	53
TC LT: 1930 only			
1930	500001	500010	10
TC YT: 1937–1938			
1937	630001	630016	16
1938	630017	630025	9
MM UT: 1936–1937 only			
1936/1937	7501	7525	25

Year	Start	End	Total
MM UTS: 1938–1957			
1938	310026	310500	475
	310626	310646	21
1939	310647	310950	304
	311151	311350	200
	311551	312450	900
1940	312751	312950	200
	313201	313550	350
	313701	314000	300
	314251	314397	147
	314401	314500	100
	314801	314892	92
1941	314893	314975	83
	315301	315450	150
	315451*	315500	50
	315501	315760	260
	315761*	315793	33
	315794	315799	6
	315800*	only	1
	316001	316294	294
	316295*	316300	6
1942	316851	317086	236
	317401	317701	301
1943	317702	318114	413
	318159	318162	4
1944	318513	318912	400
	319246	320043	798
	320094**	321013	920
1945	323172***	323647	476
	323748	324622	875
1946	327401	328250	850
	328501****	328750	250
	328751	329661	911
	329662*	329750	89
1947	332004	332919	916
	332920*	332993	74
	332994	332995	2
	332996*	333005	10
	335001	335433	433
	335434*	335443	10
	335444	335494	51
	335495*	335506	12
	335507	335554	48
	335555*	335559	5
	335560	only	1
	335561*	335565	5
	335566	335616	51
	335617*	335626	10
	335627	335782	156
	335783*	335794	12
	335795	335839	45
	335840*	335851	12
	335852	335898	47
	335899*	335910	12
	335911	only	1
	335912*	only	1
	335913	336000	88
	336451	only	1
1948	338604	338987	384
	338988*	339007	20

Year	Start	End	Total
MM UTS: 1938–1957 (continued)			
	339008	339051	44
	339052*	only	1
	339053	339058	6
	339059*	339066	8
	339067	339101	35
	339102*	339104	3
	339105	339165	61
	339166*	only	1
	339167	339181	15
	339182*	339195	14
	339196	only	1
	339197*	339199	3
	339200	only	1
	339201*	only	1
	339202	339206	5
	339207*	339214	15
	339215	only	1
	339216*	339221	6
	339222	only	1
	339223*	339225	3
	339226	339453	228
	0124800001	0124800476(*)	476
	0124800477*	0124800478	2
	0124800479	0124800491	13
	0124800492*	only	1
	0124800493	0124800494	2
	0124800495*	only	1
	0124800496	only	1
	0124800497*	only	1
	0124800498	only	1
	0124800499*	only	1
	0124800500	only	1
	0124800501*	0124800514	14
	0124800515	0124800555	41
	0124800556*	0124800562	7
	0124800563	0124800585	23
	0124800586*	only	1
	0124800587	only	1
	0124800588*	0124800591	4
	0124800592	0124800600	9
	0124800601*	only	1
	0124800602	0124800612	11
	0124800613*	0124800624	12
	0124800625	0124800650	26
	0124800651*	0124800656	6
	0124800657	0124800667	11
	0124800668*	0124800670	3
	0124800671	only cancelled	
	0124800672*	0124800686	15
	0124800687	0124800732	46
	0124800733*	0124800735	3
	0124800736	only cancelled	
	0124800737*	0124800743	7
	0124800744	0124800994	251
	0124800995*	0124801009	15
	0124801010	0124801053	44
	0124801054*	only	1
	0124801055	only	1
	0124801056*	0124801075	20

Year	Start	End	Total
MM UTS: 1938–1957 (continued)			
	0124801076	0124801114	39
	0124801115*	0124801127	13
	0124801128	0124801133	6
	0124801134*	0124801142	9
	0124801143	0124801164	22
	0124801165*	only	1
	0124801166	0124801206	41
	0124801207*	0124801220	14
	0124801221	0124801243	23
	0124801244*	0124801249	6
	0124801250	0124801254	5
	0124801255*	only	1
	0124801256	0124801257	2
	0124801258*	only	1
	0124801259	only	1
	0124801260*	0124801264	5
	0124801265	0124801274	10
	0124801275*	0124801279	5
	0124801280	0124801293	14
	0124801294*	0124801297	4
	0124801298	0124801309	12
	0124801310*	0124801313	4
	0124801314	0124801327	14
	0124801328*	0124801334	7
	0124801335	0124801359	25
	0124801360*	0124801365	6
	0124801366	0124801440	75
	0124801441*	0124801447	7
	0124801448	0124801456	9
	0124801457*	0124801463	7
	0124801464	0124801497	34
	0124801498*	0124801503	6
	0124801504	0124801511	8
	0124801512*	0124801518	7
	0124801519	0124801570	52
	0124801571*	0124801574	4
	0124801575	only	1
	0124801576*	0124801577	2
	0124801578	0124801579	2
	0124801580*	only	1
	0124801581	0124801586	6
	0124801587*	0124801591	5
	0124801592	0124801642	51
	0124801643*	0124801651	9
	0124801652	0124802276	625
1949 (**)	0124900001	0124903901	3,901
1950	0125000001	01203850	3,850
1951	01203851	01207138	3,288
1952	01207139	01210570	3,432
1953	01210571	01213219	2,648
1954	01213220	01213325	106
1955	01213326	01214125	800
1956	01214126(***)	01215100	975
1957	01215101	01215150	50

* Butane tractors
**Fender change—last of crown fenders
***Fender change—first of clamshell fenders
****Transmission bundle 2819x shipped to Sale-Tilney firm in England

(*)This number, and after, changed to the 283A-4 engine
(**)Serial number lists no longer specified fuel type
(***)From this number, and after, all UTS production is UTS Specials

MM UDLX: 1938 only

Year	Start	End	Total
1938—early	310001*	310025	25
1938—late	310501	310625	125

*Most, if not all, the first 25 units have UTX stamped on the serial number plate

MM UTU: 1939–1955

Year	Start	End	Total
1939	310951	311150	200
	311351	311550	200
1940	312451	312750	300
	312951	313200	250
	313551	313700	150
	314001	314250	250
	314501	314800	300
1941	315001	315300	300
	315801	316000	200
	316301	316500	200
1942	316501	316850	350
	317101	317400	300
1943	318115	318158	44
1944	318163	318512	350
	318913	319245	333
1945	321124**	321959	836
	321962	323171	1,210
	324749	325212	464
	325214***	325230	17
1946	325231	325698	468
	325799	327398	1,600
1947	329752	331625	1,874
	331626(*)	331652	27
	331653	only	1
	331654*	331753	100
	334001(**)	334779	779
	334780*	only	1
	334781	334798	18
	334799*	334826	28
	334827	334829	3
	334830*	334939	110
	334940	334971	32
	334972*	335000	29
	336452	337170	719
	337171*	337178	8
	337179	only	1
	337180*	only	1
	337181	337182	2
	337183*	337187	5
	337188	337233	46
	337234*	237249	16
	337250	337294	45
	337295*	337312	18
	337313	337417	105
1948	337418	337474	57
	337475*	337489	15
	337490	337536	47
	337537*	337551	15
	337552	337603	52

Year	Start	End	Total
MM UTU: 1939–1955 (continued)			
	337604*	337623	20
	337624	337663	40
	337664*	337679	16
	337680	337721	42
	337722*	337736	15
	337737	only	1
	337738*	337740	3
	337741	337783	43
	337784*	337799	16
	337800	337843	44
	337844*	337860	17
	337861	337904	44
	337905*	337924	20
	337925	337964	40
	337965*	337979	15
	337980	338035	56
	338036*	only	1
	338037	338042	6
	338043*	338046	4
	338047	338051	5
	338052	338053	canceled
	338054****	338103	50 ****
	338104(***)	338603	500 (***)
	0114800001	0114800313	313
	0114800314*	0114800328	15
	0114800329	0114800353	25
	0114800354*	only	1
	0114800355	0114800357	3
	0114800358*	0114800364	7
	0114800365	only	1
	0114800366*	0114800370	5
	0114800371	0114800422	52
	0114800423*	0114800437	15
	0114800438	0114800477	40
	0114800478*	0114800488	11
	0114800489	only	1
	0114800490*	0114800500	11
	0114800501	0114800542	42
	0114800543*	0114800563	21
	0114800564	0114800605	42
	0114800606*	0114800620	15
	0114800621	0114800713	93
	0114800714*	0114800736	23
	0114800737	only	1
	0114800738*	only	1
	0114800739	0114800778	40
	0114800779*	0114800798	20
	0114800799	0114801201	403
	0114801202*	only	1
	0114801203	0114801952	750
	0114801953*	0114802052	100
	0114802053	only	1
1949(x)	0114900001	0114900050	50(****)
	0114900051	0114905000	4,950
1950	0115000001	01105383	5,383
1951	01105384	01110117	4,734
1952	01110118	01113449	3,332
1954	01113450	01113453	4
1955	01113454	01113456	3

Year	Start	End	Total

*Butane tractors
**Fender change
***Serial number 325213 is missing
****Transmission returned from England and renumbered 00114900001-0114900050
(*)Equipped with hydraulic lifts and distributor ignitions
(**)Changed to Type 238A-4 engine
(***)Transmissions shipped to Sale-Tilney firm in England
(****)Renumbered transmissions returned from England
(x)Serial number lists no longer specified what fuel

MM UTC: 1945–1955

Year	Start	End	Total
1945	321960	321961	2
	324623	324647	25
1946	328251	328295	45
	328296	328300*	5
1947	336001	336100	100
1948	0154800001	0154800300**	300
1949	0154900001	0154900100**	100
1951	01500101	01500180**	80
1952	01500181	01500265**	85
1954	01500266	01500271**	6
	08800001	08800060***	60
1955	08800061	08800110***	50

*Converted to UTIL
**6-volt ignition
***12-volt ignition

MM UTN: 1950–1952

Year	Start	End	Total
1950	0385000001	0385000101	101
1951	03800102	03800204	103
1952	03800205	03800354	150

MM UTE: 1951–1954

Year	Start	End	Total
1951	04300001	04300111	111
1952	04300112	04300261	150
1953	04300262	04300264	3
1954	04300265	only	1

MM UTS Diesel: 1952–1956

Year	Start	End	Total
1952	05000001	05000018*	18
1954	05000019	05000755	737
1955	05000955	05001154	200
1956	05002105**	05002404	300

*Experimental or prototype tractors
**From this number, and after, all UTS Diesel production is UTS Diesel Special

MM UTSD-M: 1954–1958

Year	Start	End	Total
1954	05000756	05000954	199
1955	05001155	05002104	950
1956	10800001	10800245	245
1957	10800246	10800390	145
1958	10800391	10800550	160

MM UTSG: 1950–1951

Year	Start	End	Total
1950	0395000001	0395000050	50
1951	03900051	03900100	50

MM UDU Diesel: 1952–1953*

Year	Start	End	Total
1952	04900001	only	1
1953	04900002	04900030	29

*Experimental or prototype tractors—real production of diesel row-crop tractors began with UBU models.

MM UBU: 1953–1955

Year	Start	End	Total
1953	05800001	05802912	2,912
1954	05802913	05804002	1,090
1955	05804003	05805077	1,075

MM UBE: 1953–1955

Year	Start	End	Total
1953	05900001	05900896	896
1954	05900897	05901068	172
1955	05901069	05901421	353

MM UBN: 1953–1955

Year	Start	End	Total
1953	06000001	06000202	202
1954	06000203	06000207	5
1955	06000208	06000241	34

MM UBU Diesel: 1954–1955

Year	Start	End	Total
1954	07800001	07800746	746
1955	07800747	07801041	295

MM UBE Diesel: 1954–1955

Year	Start	End	Total
1954	07000001	07000231	231
1955	07000232	07000362	131

MM UBN Diesel: 1954 only

Year	Start	End	Total
1954	06900001	06900048	48

MM UB Special: 1955 only

Year	Start	End	Total
1955	09700001	09701475	1,475

MM UB Diesel Special: 1955–1957

Year	Start	End	Total
1955	09800001	09800300	300
1956	09800301	09800464	164
1957	09800465	09800520	56

MM UTI: 1940–1956

Year	Start	End	Total
1940	314398	314400	3*
1941	314976	314999	24
1942	317087	317100	14
1944	320044	320093	50
	321014	321101	88
1945	321102	321123	22
	323648	323747	100
	324648	324748	101
1946	325699	325798	100
	327399	327400	2
	328301	328500	198****
	329751	only	1
1947	331754	332003	250
	336101**	336450	350
1948	339454	339682	229
1949	0134900001	0134900088	88
1951	01300090	01300119	30
1952	01300120	01300139	20
1953	01300140	01300141	2
	07200001***	07200016	16
1954	07200017	07200035	19
1956	07200036	07200123	88
	07200124	07200173	50

*Prototypes with KEC engine
**Changed to Type 283A-4 engine

***Prefix 072 indicated a change to Type 283B-4 engine and 12-volt ignition
****Two tractors, serial numbers 328328-328329, were converted to UTIL

MM UTID Diesel: 1954–1955

Year	Start	End	Total
1954	05200001	only	1
1955	05200002	05200006	5

MM UTIL: 1946-1957

Year	Start	End	Total
1946	328328	328329	2***
1948	0144800001*	0144800200	200
1949	0144900001	0144900340	340
1951	01400341	01400381	41
1952	01400382	01400547	166
1953	01400548	01400573	26
	07100001**	07100134	134
1954	07100135	07100203	69
1955	07100204	07100253	50
1956	07100254	07100426	173
1957	07100427	07100635	209
1958	07100636	07100744	109
1959	07100745	07100884	140

*Prefix 014 indicates Type 283A-4 engine
**Prefix 071 indicates Type 283B-4 engine and 12-volt ignition
***Converted from UTC

MM UTIL-D: 1953–1959

Year	Start	End	Total
1953	05300001	05300002	2
1954	05300003	05300027	25
1955	05300028	only	1
1956	05300029	05300050	22
1957	05300051	05300069	19
1958	05300070	05300092	23
1959	05300093	05300114	22

MM UTIL-M: 1953 only

Year	Start	End	Total
1953	07900001	07900002*	2
	05400001	05400355	355**

*With 12-volt ignition
**All serial numbers produced with 6-volt ignition

MM UMIL: 1953 only

Year	Start	End	Total
1953	05700001	05700042	42

MM ZTU: 1936-1948

Year	Start	End	Total
1936	560001	560037	37
1937	560038	562974	2,937
1938	562975	565406	2,432
1939	565407	567154	1,748
1940	567155	567769	615
	567770*	only	
	567771	567776	6
	567777**	only	
	567778***	only	
	567779	567804	26
	567806	568017	212
	568018(*)	only	
	568019	568161	143
	568163	568487	325

Year	Start	End	Total
	568490	568555	66
	568557	568596	40
	568598	568747	150
	568749	568754	6
1941	568755	569104	350
	569105	569125	21(**)
	569126	569160	35
	569162	569167	6
	569169	569173	5
	569175	569176	2
	569178	569310	133
	569313	569322	10
	569325	569355	31
	569357	569390	34
	569392	569490	99
	569492	only	1
	569494	569495	2
	569497	569605	9
	569607	569777	71
	569779	569832	54
	569834	570478	645
	570481	570664	184
	570666	570731	66
	570733	570749	17
	570751	570752	2
	570754	570759	6
	570761	570800	40
	570802	only	1
	570805	570808	4
1942	570822	571421	600
1943	571422	572967	1,546
1944	572968	573467	500
	573584	575712	2,129
1945	575713	576813	1,101
1946	576814	577913(***)	1,100
1947	578014	579713	1,700
	579814	580801	988
	580814	581814	1,001
1948	581815	583414	1,600
	583815	583817	3
	584218	585817	1,600

*Changed to ZTS serial number 610885
**Changed to ZTS serial number 610886
***Changed to ZTS serial number 610887
(*)Scrapped 9-10-40
(**)Converted from ZTS
(***)Tractors equipped with distributor ignition, lights, starter, and battery sometime within these numbers

MM ZTN: 1940–1948

Year	Start	End	Total
1940	567805	only	1
	568162	only	1
	568488	568489	2
	568556	only	1
	568597	only	1
	568748	only	1
1941	569161	only	1
	569168	only	1
	569174	only	1

Year	Start	End	Total
	569177	only	1
	569311	569312	2
	569323	569324	2
	569356	only	1
	569391	only	1
	569491	only	1
	569493	only	1
	569496	only	1
	569606	only	1
	569778	only	1
	569833	only	1
	570479	570480	2
	570665*	only	1
	570801**	only	1
	570803**	only	1
	570804**	only	1
	570809	570821	13
1944	573468	573583	116
1946	577914	578013***	100
1947	579714	579813	100
1948	583715	583814	100

*Converted from ZTU 2-12-42
**Converted from ZTU 1-28-42
***Equipped with distributor ignition, lights, starter, and battery sometime during these serial numbers

MM ZTE: 1947—1948

Year	Start	End	Total
1947	580802	580813	12
1948	583415	583714	300
	583818	584217	400

MM ZTS: 1937–1947

Year	Start	End	Total
1937	610001	610035	35
1938	610036	610388	353
1939	610389	610684	296
1940	610685	611087	403
1941	611088	611341	254
	611342*	only	1
1942	611347	611446**	100
1943	611447	611965	519
1944	611966	612485	520
1945	612486	612885	400
1946	612886	613085	200
1947	613086	613490	405

*Converted from ZTU 12-18-41
**These tractors built 7-28-42 through 7-30-42

MM ZTI: 1936–1942

Year	Start	End	Total
1936	599001	599003	3
1937	599004	599016	13
1938	599017	599018	2
1939	599019	599022	4
1941	599023	N/A	N/A
1942	611345*	only	1
	611344**	only	1
	611346***	only	1
	611343****	only	1

*Converted from ZTU serial number 570732
**Converted from ZTU serial number 570750
***Converted from ZTU serial number 570753
****Converted from ZTU serial number 570760

MM ZTX: 1943 only

Year	Start	End	Total
1943	201	225	25

MM ZAN: 1949–1953

Year	Start	End	Total
1949	0084900001	0084900150	150
1950	0085000001	00800238	238
1951	00800239	00800442	204
1952	00800443	00800618	176
1953	00800619	00800620	2

MM ZAE: 1949–1953

Year	Start	End	Total
1949	0094900001	0094900301	301
1950	0095000001	00900373	373
1951	00900374	00900576	203
1952	00900577	00900997	421
1953	00900998	00901122	125

MM ZAU: 1949–1952

Year	Start	End	Total
1949	0064900001	0064903013	3,013
1950	0065000001	00605435	5,435
1951	00605436	00609939	4,504
1952	00609940	00614658	4,719

MM ZAS:1949–1953

Year	Start	End	Total
1949	0074900001	0074900150	150
1950	0075000001	00700480	480
1951	00700481	00701285	805
1952	00701286	00701910	625
1953	00701911	00702610	700

MM ZASI: 1952 only

Year	Start	End	Total
1952	05100001*	05100515*	515

*These are engine numbers—tractor serial numbers aren't available. The prefix for these tractors is 046.

MM ZM: 1953–1954

Year	Start	End	Total
1953	07600001	07600017	17
1954	07600018	N/A	N/A

MM ZBU: 1953–1955

Year	Start	End	Total
1953	06200001	06200957	957
1954	06200958	06202479	1,522
1955	06202480	06203059	580

MM ZBE: 1953–1955

Year	Start	End	Total
1953	06300001	06300075	75
1954	06300076	06300306	231
1955	06300307	06300501	195

MM ZBN: 1954–1955

Year	Start	End	Total
1954	06400001	06400072	72
1955	06400073	06400106	34

MM RT*: 1939–1942

Year	Start	End	Total
1939	400001	402200	2,200
1940	403801	404700	900
1942	408751	408819	69

*MHS serial number list breaks the RT out separately; however, collectors assume these to be mostly the same as RTU tractors.

Year	Start	End	Total
MM RTU: 1940–1954			
1940	402201	402800	60
	403001	403600	600
	404801	404824	24
	404826	405046	221
	405048	405090	43
	405092	405110	19
	405112	405116	5
	405118	405123	6
	405125	405140*	19
	405142	405173	32
	405175	405190	16
	405192	405212	21
	405214	405220	7
	405223	405550	328
1941	405601	406119	519
	406122	406260	139
	406269	406310	42
	406312	406332	21
	406338	406339	2
	406348	406420	73
	406443	only	1
	406446	406500	55
	406501	406615	115
	406621	407024	404
	407026	407052	27
	407054	407093	40
	407095	407103	9
	407105	407106	2
	407108	407119	12
	407121	407245	133
	407301	407414	114
	407416	only	1
	407418	407691	274
	407693	407728	36
	407730	407734	5
	407737	407750	14
	407752	407754	3
	407756	407764	9
	407766	407785	20
	407787	407937	151
1942	407951	408006	56
	408008	408020	13
	408026	408049	24
	408050**	only	1
	408051	408070	20
	408074	408120	47
	408125	408154	30
	408159	408251	93
	408259	408271	13
	408276	408300	25
	408303	408308	6
	408312	408327	16
	408330	408454	125
	408462	only	1
	408464	408526	63
	408541	408742	202
	408749	408750	2
1943	408826	409257	432
1944	409358	409898	541

Year	Start	End	Total
MM RTU: 1940–1954 (continued)			
	409950	410255	306
	410406	410747	342
1945	410748	411900	1,153
	412156	413255	1,100
	413356	413655	300
1946	413856	414455***	600
	414456****	415155	700
	415456	416455	1,000
1947	416756	418456	1,701
	418957	420244	1,288
	420657	422057	1,401
1948	0014800001	0014802402	2,402
1949	0014900001	0014903039	3,039
1950	0015000001	0015002155	2,155
1951	00102156	00103972	1,817
1952	00103973	00104823	851
1954	00104824	00104831	8

*Serial number 405138 was converted to an experimental RTI

**Shipped to engineering

***Equipped with magneto ignition—all prior RTU tractors were equipped with magneto ignition

****This serial number, and after, changed to distributor ignition, lights, starter, and battery

Year	Start	End	Total
MM RTN: 1940–1951			
1940	402801	403000	200
1941	406120N*	406121N	2
	406261N	406268N	8
	406311N	only	1
	406333N	406337N	5
	406340N	406347N	8
	406439N	only	1
	406616N	406620N	5
	407025N	only	1
	407053N	only	1
	407094N	only	1
	407104N	only	1
	407107N	only	1
	407120N	only	1
	407415N	only	1
	407417N	only	1
	407736N***	only	1
	407765N***	only	1
1942	408007N	only	1
	408021N	408025N	5
	408071N	408073N	3
	408121N	408124N	4
	408155N	408158N	4
	408252N	408258N	7
	408272N	408275N	4
	408301N	408302N	2
	408309N**	408311	3
	408328	408329	2
	408455	408461	7
	408463	only	1
	408527	408540	14
	408743	408748	6
1944	410281	410305	25

Year	Start	End	Total
MM RTN: 1940–1951 (continued)			
1945	411901	411905	5
1946	415156	415255	100
1947	418457	418656	200
1948	0034800001	0034800100	100
1949	0034900001	0034900200	200
1950	0035000001	0035000093	93
1951	00300094	00300173	80

*Beginning with this serial number, until late in 1942 production, an "N" suffix is listed on the serial number

**Last serial number with "N" suffix

***Converted from RTU on 10-8-41

Year	Start	End	Total
MM RTS: 1940–1953			
1940*	403601	403699(*)	99
	403700	403799**	
	403800	only	1
	404701	404800	100
1941	406421	406438	18
	406440	406442	3
	406444	406445	2
	407246	407300	55
	407692***	only	1
	407729***	only	1
	407735***	only	1
	407751***	only	1
	407755***	only	1
	407786***	only	1
	407938	407950	13
1944	409899	409949	51
	410256	410280	25
1945	411906	412155	250
1946	416456	416544	89
1947	416545	416605	61
	420245	420444	200
1949	0024900001	0024900375	375
1950	0025000001	0025000300	300
1951	00200301	00200401	101
1952	00200402	00200551	150
1953	00200552	00200701	150

*It is believed that a small number of RTS tractors were produced in 1939

**These serial numbers were canceled and never used

***Converted from RTU on 10-3-41

(*)Serial number 403676S was converted to an experimental RTI—5-1-40

Year	Start	End	Total
MM RTE: 1947–1953			
1947	420845	420856	12
1948	0044800001	0044800501	501
1949	0044900001	0044900315	315
1950	0045000001	0045000204	204
1951	00400205	00400281	77
1952	00400282	only	1
1953	00400283	00400287	5

Year	Start	End	Total
MM RTI: 1940–1955			
1940	404825	only	1
	405047	only	1
	405091	only	1
	405111	only	1

MM RTI: 1940–1955 (continued)

Year	Start	End	Total
	405117	only	1
	405124	only	1
	405141	only	1
	405174	only	1
	405191	only	1
	405213	only	1
	405221	only	1
	405551	405575	25
1941	405576	405600	25
1943	409258	409307*	50
	409308**	409357	50
1944	410306	410405	100
1945	413256	413355	100
	413656	413754	99
1946	413755	413855***	101
	415256****	415455	200
1947	416606	416755	150
	418657	418956	300
	420445	420844	400
1948	0054800001	0054800700	700
1949	0054900001	0054900450	450
1950	0055000001	0055000115	115
1951	00500116	00500598	483
1952	00500599	00501000	402
1953	00501001	00501311	311
1954	00501312	00501511	200
1955	00501512	00501579	68

*Equipped with light axle, this serial number and before
**Equipped with heavy axle from this point on
***Up to this serial number the RTI was equipped with magneto ignition
****This serial number, and after, equipped with distributor ignition, lights, starter, and battery

MM RTI-M: 1953 only

Year	Start	End	Total
1953	05500001	05500249	249

MM GT/GTS: 1938–1941

Year	Start	End	Total
1938	160007	160076	70
1939	160077	160545	469
	160557	160579	23
1940	160580*	160878	292
1941	160879	161206	328
	161235	161253	19

*Serial numbers 160633 through 160639 were canceled

MM GTI: 1938–1941

Year	Start	End	Total
1938	160001	160006	6*
1940	160546	160556	11
1941	161207	161234	28

*Special GT Industrial tractors for Grader conversions

MM GTA: 1942–1947

Year	Start	End	Total
1942	162001	162300	300
1943	162301	162302	2
1944	162303	162659	357
1945	162660	162869	210
1946	162870	163079	210
	163110	163203	94

MM GTA: 1942–1947 (continued)

Year	Start	End	Total
	163210	163219	10
1947	163220	163610	391

MM GTA Industrial: 1946 only

Year	Start	End	Total
1946	163080	163109	30*
	163204	163209	6**

*Gasoline tractors
**LP gas tractors

MM GTB: 1947–1954

Year	Start	End	Total
1947	164001	164138	138
	164140	164175	36
	164177	164178	2
1948	164139	only	1
	164176	only	1
	164179	164214	36
	0164800001	0164800600	600
1949	0164900001	016491205	1,205
1950	0165000001	01601863	1,863
1951	01601864	01603396	1,533
1952	01603397	01604889	1,493
1953	01604890	01605972	1,083
1954	01605973	01606289	317

MM GTB-D: 1953–1954

Year	Start	End	Total
1953	06800001	only	1
1954	06800002	06800850	849

MM GTC LP gas: 1951–1953

Year	Start	End	Total
1951	04700001	04700018	18
1952	04700019	04700676	658
1953	04700677	04701101	1,082

MM GB: 1955–1959

Year	Start	End	Total
1955	08900001	08901500	1,500
1956	08901501	08902601	1,101
1957	08902602	08903401	800
1958	08903402	08904251	850
1959	08904252	08904492	241

MM GB-Diesel: 1955–1959

Year	Start	End	Total
1955	09000001	09000850	850
1956	09000851	09001525	675
1957	09001526	09002145	620
1958	09002146	09002655	510
1959	09002656	09002790	135

Massey-Ferguson MF-95: 1958–1959

Year	Start	End	Total
1958	15600001	15600450	450
1959	15600451	15601100	650

MM UTX: 1941

Year	Start	End	Total
1941	X143	experimental	1
	X158*	experimental	1
	X159	experimental	1
	X160	experimental	1
	X170	experimental	1
	X176	experimental	1

*Built 10-29-1941 with KEF engine number 547178

MM NTX: 1942–1944

Year	Start	End	Total
1942	2501	2663	163
1943	2664	2964	301
	2965	3023*	
	3024	3134	111
1944	3135	3157	23
	3158	3190*	
	3191	3440	250
	3441	3502*	
	3503	3504**	
			***

*Spare transmissions for NTX
**Spare transmissions for repairs
***The U.S. Navy accepted 840 NTX tractors

MM GTX: 1942–1944

Year	Start	End	Total
1942	175001M	175023M	23
1943	175060M	175101M	42
1944	175102M	175120M	19

MM Crash Crane: 1944 only

Year	Start	End	Total
1944	CN1	CN20	20

Avery Louisville Motor Plow: 1914–1917

Year	Start	End	Total
1914–1917	N/A	N/A	N/A

Avery A: 1943–1950

Year	Start	End	Total
1943-1944	*1FA000	4A785	4,785
1945	4A786	7A304	2,519
1946	7A305	9A866	2,562
1947	9A867	13A246	3,380
1948	13A247	17A455	4,209
1949	17A456	19A365	1,910
1950	19A366	20A114	749

*The prefix number designates 1000s

Avery V: 1946–1952

Year	Start	End	Total
1946	*1V5	1V143	1,139
1947	1V144	2V576	2,433
1948	2V577	4V489	1,913
1949	4V490	5V500	1,011
1950	5V501	6V206	706
1951	6V207	6V421	215
1952	6V422	7V271	850

*The prefix number designates 1000s

Avery/MM R: 1950–1951

Year	Start	End	Total
1950	R500	R1838	1,339
1951	R1839	R4459	2,621

Avery/MM BF: 1952*

Year	Start	End	Total
1952	R4460	R6537	2,078

*Sometime during 1952 the color was changed from Avery red to MM Prairie Gold

MM BFW: 1953

Year	Start	End	Total
1953	R6538	R7571	1,034

MM BFD: 1953

Year	Start	End	Total
1953	57700001	57700358	358

MM BFS: 1953

Year	Start	End	Total
1953	57600001	57600047	47

Year	Start	End	Total
MM BFH: 1953			
1953	58000001	58000150	150
MM BG: 1953–1955			
1953	57900001	57900600	600
1954	57900601	57900768	168
1955	57900769	57901200	432
MM Uni-Tractor: 1951–1963			
1951	75700001	75700254	254
1952	75700255	75701070	816
1953	75701071	75703118	2,048
1954	75703119	75704118	1,000
1955	08704119	08705418	1,300
1956	08705419	08706418	1,000
1957	08706419	08707687	1,269
1958	08707688	08708062	375
1959	08708063	08708488	426
1960	42200001	42200637	637
1961	42200638	42201134	497
1962	42201135	42201637	503
	42201638	42201663	26*
1963	42201664	42201683	20*

*Produced for the Government Chemical Corps

Year	Start	End	Total
MM 335 Utility: 1956–1961			
1956	10400001	10400101	101
1957	10400102	10402087	1,986
1958	10402088	10402336	249
1959	10402337	10402439	103
1960	10402440	10402489	50
1961	10402490	10402539	50
MM 335 Universal: 1957–1959			
1957	11600001	11600301	301
1958	11600302	11600305	4
1959	11600306	11600334	29
MM 335 Industrial: 1957–1960			
1957	11300001	11300440	440
1958	11300441	11300521	81
1959	11300522	11300596	75
1960	11300597	11300746	150
MM 445 Utility: 1956–1959			
1956	10200001	10201445	1,445
1957	10201446	10202101	656
1958	10202102	10202242	141
1959	10202243	10202249	7
MM 445 Utility Diesel: 1959 only			
1959	15400001	15400018	18
MM 445 Universal: 1956–1959			
1956	10100001	10102854	2,854
1957	10102855	10104125	1,271
1958	10104126	10104804	679
1959	10104805	10104847	43
MM 445 Universal Diesel: 1958 only			
1958	15200001	15200190	190

Year	Start	End	Total
MM 445 Industrial: 1956–1958			
1956	11100001	11100075	75
1957	11100076	11100388	313
1958	11100389	11100645	257
MM 445 Industrial Diesel: 1958 only			
1958	15300001	15300025	25
MM 445 Military: 1958 only			
1958	15700001	15700074	74
MM 445 Crawler: 1956			
1956	X253	experimental	1
MM 2 Star Crawler: 1958 only			
1958	12000001	12000051	51
MM Motrac Crawler: 1960–1961			
1960	18500001	18500030	30
1961	18500031	18500038	8
MM Motrac Diesel Crawler: 1960–1961			
1960	18600001	18600160	160
1961	18600161	only	1
MM BIG MO 400: 1961–1964			
1961	16700001	16700100	100
1962	16700101	16700210	110
1963	16700211	16700360	150
1964	16700361	16700410	50
MM BIG MO 400 Military: 1959–1963			
1959	17000001	17000356	356
1960	17000357	17000632	276
1961	17000633	17000648	16
1962	17000649	17000652	4
1963	17000653	17000757	105
MM BIG MO 500: 1960–1966			
1960	16800001	16800160	160
1961	16800161	16800391	231
1962	16800392	16800606	215
1963	16800607	16800681	75
1964	16800682	16800746	65
1965	16800747	16800866	120
1966	16800867	16800881	15
MM BIG MO 500 Diesel: 1960–1965			
1960	17800001	17800065	65
1963	17800066	17800090	25
1964	17800091	17800115	25
1965	17800116	17800145	30
MM BIG MO 600: 1960 only			
1960	18400001	18400060	60
MM Jet Star:* 1959–1962			
1959	16500001	16500284	284
1960	16500285	16500834	550
1961	16500835	16501701	867
1962	16501702	16502439	738

*Some of these tractors became Boozer Orchard conversions

Year	Start	End	Total
MM Jet Star Diesel: 1960–1962			
1960	17500001	17500060	60
1961	17500061	17500135	75
1962	17500136	17500196	61
MM Jet Star Orchard: 1961 only			
1961	22000001	22000050	50
MM Jet Star 2 Gasoline or LP gas: 1963 only			
1963	25800001	25801100	1,100
MM Jet Star 2 Diesel: 1963 only			
1963	25700001	25700113	113
MM Jet Star 2 Orchard Gasoline or LP gas: 1963 only			
1963	22000051	22000072*	22

*Possible that there were more produced but this is the last serial number we can verify

Year	Start	End	Total
MM Jet Star 2 Orchard Diesel: 1963 only			
1963	26300001	N/A*	N/A*

*Records don't give us these numbers but collectors believe that less than 10 were produced.

Year	Start	End	Total
MM Jet Star 3 Gasoline or LP gas: 1964–1965			
1964	28300001	28301000	1,000
1965	28301001	28301984	984
MM Jet Star 3 Super* Gasoline or LP gas: 1965–1970			
1965	28301985	28302055	71
1966	28302056	28302843	788
1967	28302844	28304155**	1,312
1968	28304156	28304800	645
1969	28304801	28305085	285
1970	28305086	28305335	250

*These numbers include the Cockshutt Model 1350 production

**Tractors with serial numbers 28303561 through 28303565 had 220A-4 engines

Year	Start	End	Total
MM Jet Star 3 Diesel and Super Diesel: 1964–1970			
1964	28400001	28400050	50
1965	28400051	28400200	150
1966	28400201	28400385	185
1967	28400386	28400466	81
1968	28400467	28400526	60
1969	28400527	28400601	75
1970	28400602	28400711	110
MM Jet Star 3 Super LP gas: 1970			
1970	36000001	36000010	10
MM Jet Star 3 Super Diesel Orchard: 1967 only			
1967	34400001	34400020	20

Year	Start	End	Total

MM Jet Star 3* Orchard LP gas: 1965–1967

Year	Start	End	Total
1965	30700001	30700050	50
1966	30700051	only	1
1967	30700052	30700070	19

*Jet Star 3 Super Orchard tractors are included within these serial numbers—probably during 1967.

Cockshutt Model 1350: 1966–1968

Year	Start	End	Total
1966	28302844	28302893	50
1967	28303141	28303390	250
1968	28304546	28304625	80

MM Jet Star 3 Industrial gasoline: 1966–1967

Year	Start	End	Total
1966	30800001	3080156	156
1967	30800157	30800191	35

MM Jet Star 3 Industrial Diesel: 1966 only

Year	Start	End	Total
1966	30900001	30900050	50

MM 4 Star Gasoline and LP gas: 1959–1963

Year	Start	End	Total
1959	16600001	16600890	890
1960	16600891	16601685	795
1961	16601686	16601860	175
1962	16601861	16602407	547
1963	16602408	16602537	130

MM 4 Star Diesel: 1960–1962

Year	Start	End	Total
1960	18200001	18200050	50
1961	18200051	18200072	22
1962	18200073	18200097	25

MM U302: 1964–1965

Year	Start	End	Total
1964	27600001	27601000	1,000
1965	27601001	27601300	300

MM U302 Super: 1966–1970

Year	Start	End	Total
1966	27601301	27602300	1,000
1967	27602301	27602425	125
1968	27602426	27602759	334
1969	27602760	27602859	100
1970	27602860	27602969	110

MM U302 Super Diesel: 1967–1970

Year	Start	End	Total
1967	27700001	27700100	100
1968	27700101	27700150	50
1969	27700151	27700164	14
1970	27700165	27700190	26

MM U302 Super LP gas: 1969–1970

Year	Start	End	Total
1969	36100001	36100025	25
1970	36100026	36100050	25

MM 5 Star Standard: 1958 only

Year	Start	End	Total
1958	11200001	11200380	380

MM 5 Star Standard Diesel: 1958–1959

Year	Start	End	Total
1958	14500001	14500165	165
1959	14500166	14500188	23

MM 5 Star Universal: 1957–1959

Year	Start	End	Total
1957	11000001	11001057	1,057
1958	11001058	11002067*	1,003
1959	11002068	11002914	847

*Serial numbers 11002061 through 11002067 were canceled and not used

MM 5 Star Universal Diesel: 1957–1959

Year	Start	End	Total
1957	14400001	14400203	203
1958	14400204	14400785	582
1959	14400786	14401295	510

MM 5 Star Industrial: 1957–1959

Year	Start	End	Total
1957	11700002	11700006	5
1958	11700007	11700025	19
1959	11700026	11700084	59

MM 5 Star Industrial Diesel: 1958–1960

Year	Start	End	Total
1958	14600001	14600010	10
1959	14600011	14600028	18
1960	14600029	14600060	32

MM M5: 1960–1963

Year	Start	End	Total
1960	17100001	17101535	1,535
1961	17101536	17103495	1,960
1962	17103496	17104707	1,212
1963	17104708	17105157	450

MM M5 Diesel: 1960–1963

Year	Start	End	Total
1960	17200001	17201040	1,040
1961	17201041	17201999	959
1962	17202000	17202506	507
1963	17202507	17202656	150

MM M504: 1962 only

Year	Start	End	Total
1962	24300001	24300010	10

MM M504 Diesel: 1962 only

Year	Start	End	Total
1962	24200001	24200021	21

MM M602: 1963–1964

Year	Start	End	Total
1963	26600001	26601275	1,275
1964	26601276	26602957	1,682

MM M602 Diesel: 1963–1964

Year	Start	End	Total
1963	26700001	26700742	742
1964	26700743	26701772	1,030

MM M604: 1963–1964

Year	Start	End	Total
1963	26800001	26800050	50
1964	26800051	26800053	3

MM M604 Diesel: 1963–1964

Year	Start	End	Total
1963	26900001	26900050	50
1964	26900051	26900099	49

MM M670: 1964–1965

Year	Start	End	Total
1964	29900001	29900006	6
1965	29900007	29901891	1,885

MM M670 Diesel: 1964–1965

Year	Start	End	Total
1964	30000001	30000004	4
1965	30000005	30000819	815

MM M670 Super: 1966–1970

Year	Start	End	Total
1966	29901892	29903579	1,688
1967	29903580	29904454	875
1968	29904455	29904594	140
1969	29904595	29905004	410
1970	29905005	29905104	100

MM M670 Super Diesel: 1966–1970

Year	Start	End	Total
1966	30000820	30001634	815
1967	30001635	30002309	675
1968	30002310	30002569	260
1969	30002570	30002860	291
1970	30002861	30003085	225

MM M670 Super LP gas: 1970 only

Year	Start	End	Total
1970	36200001	36200075	75

MM GVI: 1959–1962

Year	Start	End	Total
1959	16000001	16000876	876
1960	16000877	16001675	799
1961	16001676	16002032	357
1962	16002033	16002352	320

Massey-Ferguson MF 95 Super: 1961–1962

Year	Start	End	Total
1961	21200001	21200050	50
1962	21200051	21200100	50

MM GVI Diesel: 1959–1962

Year	Start	End	Total
1959	16200001	16200805	805
1960	16200806	16201890	1,085
1961	16201891	16202960	1,070
1962	16202961	16203235	275

Massey-Ferguson MF 95 Super Diesel: 1960–1962

Year	Start	End	Total
1960	17300001	17300700	700
1961	17300701	17301350	650
1962	17301351	17301775	425

MM G704: 1962 only

Year	Start	End	Total
1962	23400001	23400081	81

MM G704 Diesel: 1962 only

Year	Start	End	Total
1962	23500001	23500123	123

Massey-Ferguson MF 95 Super Diesel 4WD: 1962 only

Year	Start	End	Total
1962	24900001	24900050	50

MM G705 LP gas: 1962–1965

Year	Start	End	Total
1962	23800001	23800078	78
1963	23800079	23800590	512
1964	23800591	23801092	502
1965	23801093	23801223	131

Massey-Ferguson MF 97:* 1962–1963

Year	Start	End	Total
1962	25300001	25300095	95
1963	25300096	25300435	340

*Massey-Ferguson serial numbers include both the two-wheel-drive and front-wheel-assist models in LP gas

Year	Start	End	Total

MM G705 Diesel: 1962–1965

Year	Start	End	Total
1962	23900001	23900050	50
1963	23900051	23900898	848
1964	23900899	23901868	970
1965	23901869	23902094	226

Massey-Ferguson MF 97 Diesel:* 1962–1965

1962	25200001	25200505	505
1963	25200506	25202204	1,699
1964	25202205	25203569	1,365
1965	25203570	25203665	96

*Massey-Ferguson serial numbers include both the two-wheel-drive and front-wheel-assist diesel models

MM G706 LP gas: 1962–1965

1962	24000001	24000072	72
1963	24000073	24000305	233
1964	24000306	24000350	45
1965	24000351	24000370	20

MM G706 Diesel: 1962–1965

1962	24100001	24100106	106
1963	24100107	24100549	443
1964	24100550	24100795	246
1965	24100796	24100821	26

MM G707 LP gas: 1965 only

1965	31200001	31200283	283

MM G707 Diesel: 1965 only

1965	31300001	31300415	415

MM G708 LP gas: 1965 only

1965	31400001	31400031	31

MM G708 Diesel: 1965 only

1965	31500001	31500075	75

MM G900 LP gas and gasoline: 1967–1969

1967	33000001	33000110	110
1968	33000111	33000550	440
1969	33000551	33000670	120

MM G900 Diesel: 1967–1969

1967	33100001	33100316	316
1968	33100317	33101376*	1,060
1969	33101377	33101946	570

*25 of these serial numbers are front-wheel-assist tractors. See serial number list for G900 Diesel Front-Wheel Assist below.

MM G900 Diesel Front-Wheel Assist: 1968 only

1968	33101165	33101189	25

MM G900 LP gas: 1969 only*

1969	36300001	36300160	160

*Late in 1969 the LP gas G900 tractor was assigned separate serial numbers. Prior to this the LP gas and gasoline tractors serial numbers were not listed separately.

MM G1000 Row-crop Gasoline and LP gas: 1965–1968

1965	30500001	30500450	450
1966	30500451	30500926	476
1967	30500927	30501041	115
1968	30501042	30501051*	10

*Pilot Vistas

MM G1000 Row-crop Diesel: 1965–1968

1965	30600001	30600500	500
1966	30600501	30601125	625
1967	30601126	30601285	160
1968	30601286	30601300*	15

*Pilot Vistas

MM G1000 LP gas* Wheatland and Rice Special 1966–1969

1966	32600001	32600515	515
1967	32600516	32600650	35
1968	32600651	32600652	2
1969	32600653	32600822	170

*If gasoline models were manufactured they would fall within these serial numbers.

MM G1000* Diesel Wheatland and Rice Special: 1966–1969

1966	32700001	32700796	796
1967	32700797	32701450	654
1968	32701451	32701774	324
1969	32701775	32702050	276

*Front-wheel assist models would fall within these serial numbers.

MM G1000 Vista LP gas: 1967–1969

1967	34500011*	34500290	290
1968	34500291	34500390	100
1969	34500391	34500564	174

*First 10 were produced under prefix 305

MM G1000 Vista Diesel: 1967–1969

1967	X635	experimental	1
	34600016**	34600735	720
1968	34600736	34601185*	450
1969	34601186	34601610*	425

*Some of these serial numbers were front-wheel-assist models.

** Notes on the serial number prefix for 346 state that a pilot lot of 15 were produced under the prefix 306, which designates the G1000 Diesel.

MM G1000 Vista Diesel Front-Wheel Assist: 1968*

1968	34600961	3460985	25*

*There were more front-wheel-assist models than these numbers reflect. Actual serial numbers have been found from 34601417 through 34601431 and serial number 34601553.

MM G350* Diesel: 1971–1975

1971	302458	303466	N/A
1972	302402**	307220	N/A
1973	307221	314368	N/A
1974	314369	319893	N/A
1975	317000	321497	N/A

*These are Fiat-built tractors with Oliver Model 1265 serial numbers. To date there appear to be no records of separate MM serial numbers.

**This serial number seems to be in error—perhaps a typo when the list was compiled.

MM G450* Diesel: 1971–1975

1971	706251	712386	N/A
1972	706277**	716975	N/A
1973	714614	730076	N/A
1974	725451	764138	N/A
1975	729125	766614	N/A

* These are Fiat-built tractors with Oliver Model 1365 serial numbers. To date there appear to be no records of separate MM serial numbers.

** This serial number seems to be in error—perhaps a typo when the list was compiled.

MM G550* Diesel: 1971 only

1971	226403	230210	N/A

*Same tractor as the Oliver Model 1555 with Oliver serial numbers. To date there appear to be no records of separate MM serial numbers.

MM G750* Diesel: 1971 only

1971	225997	230735	N/A

*Same tractor as the Oliver Model 1655 with Oliver serial numbers. To date there appear to be no records of separate MM serial numbers.

MM G850* Gasoline, LP gas, Diesel: 1971 only

1971	226445	229636	N/A

*Same tractor as the Oliver Model 1755 with Oliver serial numbers. To date there appear to be no records of separate MM serial numbers.

MM G940* Diesel: 1971 only

1971	225508	231365	N/A

*Same tractor as the Oliver Model 1855 with Oliver serial numbers. To date there appear to be no records of separate MM serial numbers.

MM G950 LP gas: 1969–1971

1969	43500001	43500060	60
1970	43500061	43500085	25
1971	43500086	43500186	101

MM G950 Diesel: 1969–1972

1969	43600001	43600210	210
1970	43600211	43600415	205
1971	43600416	43600829	414
1972	43600830	43600834	5

Year	Start	End	Total
MM G1050 LP gas: 1969–1972			
1969	43000001	43000040	40
1970	43000041	43000060	20
1971	43000061	43000105	45
1972	43000106	43000111	6
MM G1050 Diesel: 1969–1971			
1969	43100001	43100285	285
1970	43100286	43100415	130
1971	43100416	43100544	129
MM G1350 Row-crop LP gas: 1969–1972			
1969	43200001	43200022	22
1970	43200023	43200044	22
1971	43200045	43200097	53
1972	43200098	43200108	11
MM G1350 Row-crop Diesel: 1970–1972			
1970	43300001	43300042	42
1971	43300043	43300253	211
1972	43300254	43300322	69

Year	Start	End	Total
MM G1350 Wheatland LP gas: 1969 only			
1969	45300001	45300005	5
MM A4T-1400 Diesel: 1969–1970			
1969	43900001	43900102	102
1970	43900103	43900247	145
MM A4T-1600 LP gas: 1970–1972			
1970	45700001	45700126	126
1971	45700127	45700197	71
1972	45700198	45700257	60
MM A4T-1600 Diesel: 1970–1972			
1970	45600001	45600187	187
1971	45600188	45600700	513
1972	45600701	45601190	490

Year	Start	End	Total
MM G955* Diesel or LP gas: 1973–1974			
1973	239825	243262	N/A
1974	244559	251357	N/A

*Serial numbers include both diesel and LP gas tractors. These are Oliver serial numbers and probably include the White 1870 production numbers. There are no records of separate MM serial numbers.

Year	Start	End	Total
MM G1355* Diesel or LP gas: 1973–1974			
1973	236440	244184	N/A
1974	245258	252710	N/A

*Serial numbers include both diesel and LP gas tractors. These are Oliver serial numbers and probably include the White 2270 production tractors. There are no records of separate MM serial numbers.

BIBLIOGRAPHY

Broehl, Wayne G. *John Deere's Company*. New York, NY: Doubleday & Company, Inc., 1984.

Dunning, Lorry. *Ultimate American Farm Tractor Data Book*. Osceola, Wisconsin: MBI Publishing Company, 1999.

Gray, R. B. *The Agricultural Tractor 1855-1950*. St. Joseph, Michigan: ASAE, 1975.

King, Alan, ed. *Minneapolis-Moline Data Book No. 2*. Delaware, Ohio: Independent Print Shop, 1988.

Larsen, Lester. *Farm Tractors 1950-1975*. St. Joseph, Michigan: ASAE, 1981.

Sayers, Al. *Minneapolis-Moline Tractors*. Osceola, Wisconsin: MBI Publishing Company, 1996.

Thomas, Norman F. *Minneapolis-Moline: A History of its Formation and Operations*. Arno Press, 1976.

Wendel, C. H. *Encyclopedia of American Farm Tractors*. Osceola, Wisconsin: MBI Publishing Company, 1992.

Wendel, C. H. *Minneapolis-Moline Tractors 1870-1969*. Osceola, Wisconsin: MBI Publishing Company, 1990.

INDEX